BASKETBALL'S
GREATEST GAMES

BASKETBALL'S
GREATEST GAMES

Edited by Zander Hollander

The Official NBA Library

An Associated Features Book

PRENTICE-HALL, INC.
Englewood Cliffs, New Jersey

Basketball's Greatest Games
edited by Zander Hollander

ISBN 0-13-072306-1
Library of Congress Catalog Card Number: 78-134685

Printed in the United States of America *T*

Prentice-Hall International, Inc., London
Prentice-Hall of Australia, Pty. Ltd., Sydney
Prentice-Hall of Canada, Ltd., Toronto
Prentice-Hall of India Private Ltd., New Delhi
Prentice-Hall of Japan, Inc., Tokyo

FOREWORD

Reading *Basketball's Greatest Games* brought back fresh memories of some games with a special significance to the National Basketball Association—Wilt Chamberlain's 100-point game, Red Auerbach's last game as coach of the Boston Celtics, and other unforgettable games in the NBA careers of Bob Pettit, Jerry West, Bob Cousy and the New York Knicks of 1970, to name just a few.

The concept that editor Zander Hollander uses in *Basketball's Greatest Games* is refreshingly different. Never before have I seen such an anthology of basketball lore brought so realistically to life. He puts the reader in the stands for the epic Houston Astrodome showdown between Lew Alcindor and Elvin Hayes. He puts the reader in the proper perspective to appreciate the first televised basketball game. And he recaptures some great collegiate moments of players who later distinguished themselves in the NBA—the Bill Bradley clash with Cazzie Russell at the old Madison Square Garden in the 1964 Holiday Festival; Wilt Chamberlain's frustrating loss to North Carolina in the 1957 NCAA tournament; and, of course, Elvin Hayes' triumph over Lew Alcindor and UCLA, only to be upstaged by a UCLA romp later in the 1968 NCAA semifinals.

The historian will appreciate Hollander's balanced menu of stories—the longest game in basketball, the biggest one-man show ever in the NBA, and Ernie Calverley's memorable 58-foot basket in the NIT.

The casual fan will also appreciate this unique collection because any of the 21 stories can be read separately and enjoyed.

The Official NBA Library is greatly enhanced by this latest volume.

Walter Kennedy
Commissioner
National Basketball Association

INTRODUCTION

Basketball's Greatest Games is the name of this book; it could also serve as the name of a parlor game for basketball fans. Try it at the next gathering of cage buffs—whether in the TV room, the corner candy store, the local watering place or the steam room of the "Y".

Hand out slips of paper to all hands and ask them to jot down what they consider the 21 greatest basketball games. Then compare the lists and enjoy the debates. If any two lists are identical, somebody was copying.

As preparation for this book, I tried the parlor game on basketball experts—coaches, players, fans from coast to coast—and what a ballgame I had. Oh, there was agreement on perhaps ten games, but after that, well, play it and see for yourself.

Ground rules: "Greatest games" were judged on the basis of historical significance; or the confrontation between two outstanding individuals or two outstanding teams; or the record-breaking—or otherwise unusual—achievements of teams or individuals. Games played before 1940 were not considered. How can anyone remember before then?

The 21 games that finally emerged reflect a mixed bag of history, including such familiar names as Alcindor, Cousy, Robertson, Bradley, Russell (Bill and Cazzie), Chamberlain, Reed, Calverley, Hayes, Baylor, West, Greer, Auerbach, Vandeweghe, Ferrin, McGuire—and among others, such teams as the New York Knickerbockers, Boston Celtics, Harlem Globetrotters, Los Angeles Lakers, Syracuse Nationals, St. Louis Hawks, Philadelphia Warriors, Minneapolis Lakers, UCLA, Princeton, North Carolina and Kansas.

For writers, I sought, wherever possible, journalists who had actually been at the game selected, or had close contact with some of the principals. I am grateful to this far-flung and distinguished lineup of contributors: John J. Archibald, St. Louis *Post-Dispatch*; Ira Berkow, Newspaper Enterprise Association; Arnie Burdick, Syracuse *Herald-Journal*; Andy Carra, *Sport* Magazine; Murray Chass, *The New York Times*; Larry Felser, Buffalo *Evening News*; Bob Fowler, St. Paul *Pioneer-Press*; Joe Gergen, *Newsday*; Jim O'Brien, New York *Post*; Steve Guback, Washington *Star*; Jack Hewins, Associated Press (Seattle); Leonard Koppett, *The New York Times*; Bill Libby; Tim Moriarty, *Newsday*; Sandy Padwe, Philadelphia *Inquirer*; Jeff Prugh, Los Angeles *Times*; Bob Sales, Boston *Globe*; David Schulz, *The Morning Telegraph*; Joseph P. Val, former sports editor of the New York *World-Telegram*; Bob Wolf, Milwaukee *Journal*.

Why 21 games? "21" was a popular schoolyard basketball game when I was a boy.

Zander Hollander
Baldwin, New York

CONTENTS

	Foreword	*Walter Kennedy*	iii
	Introduction	*Zander Hollander*	v
1	Debut of a Kid Named Lew	*Bob Wolf*	1
2	Bradley vs. Caz	*Leonard Koppett*	15
3	Wilt and Elg	*Sandy Padwe*	27
4	Big O and Big Spoon	*Ira Berkow*	35
5	The Living-Room Bounce	*Joseph P. Val*	45
6	Surprise for the Globetrotters	*Jack Hewins*	53
7	Fort Wayne Freeze	*Bob Fowler*	67
8	The Calverley Shot	*Murray Chass*	77
9	Man of the Century	*Sandy Padwe*	89
10	All-Stars' All-Star	*David Schulz*	99
11	The Longest Game	*Larry Felser*	111
12	Gun from the West	*Bill Libby*	123
13	The Last Cigar	*Bob Sales*	137
14	Champs of the Astrodome	*Jeff Prugh*	149
15	Syracuse's Easter Parade	*Arnie Burdick*	167
16	Ernie the Kid	*Tim Moriarty*	177
17	Cousy's Overtime Payoff	*Andy Carra*	187
18	Night of the Hawk	*John J. Archibald*	197
19	The Blitz Kids	*Joe Gergen*	207
20	McGuire's Yankee Rebels	*Steve Guback*	219
21	The Miracle of the Knicks	*Jim O'Brien*	231

BASKETBALL'S
GREATEST GAMES

1

DEBUT
OF A KID NAMED LEW

Bob Wolf

•

•

Under normal circumstances, October 18, 1969, would have been just another busy Saturday in the heart of the college football season. But, on this particular Saturday, Lew Alcindor was going to play his first regular-season basketball game as a professional. The occasion was deemed so important that the American Broadcasting Company had juggled its schedule so it could televise the game nationally.

Every one of the 7,782 fans in the Milwaukee Arena, and the millions more across the country, were watching to see the 7-foot-1½-inch youngster from New York in his National Basketball Association debut with the Milwaukee Bucks

3

Milwaukee's Lew Alcindor gets leverage by using the head of Detroit Piston Otto Moore in the Big A's inaugural NBA game. UPI

against the Detroit Pistons. Alcindor had been followed by pro scouts since he was in junior high school. He had attracted national attention while playing for Power Memorial Academy, and it was on nationwide television that he announced his decision to attend college at UCLA. Everything Alcindor did after that was reported by the newspapers . . . and television.

ABC usually carried the NBA games weekly—on Sunday. And its schedule usually didn't start until January, after the football season. But this time the network went to Saturday coverage in October for Lew Alcindor's inaugural. The network didn't rest on its normal game procedure. An extra camera was assigned to concentrate on Alcindor during timeouts. ABC also put in two extra rows of lights over the arena floor to bring the candlepower to the required intensity for a color telecast. The equipment, brought in all the way from New York and not just from nearby Chicago, filled three huge trucks that took up almost a city block.

That the cameras were in Milwaukee rather than in Phoenix or some other city had a lot to do with luck. Milwaukee and Phoenix were both new franchises in the NBA during the 1968–69 season and, as expected, each finished last in its respective division. The Bucks had the better record, but by prior agreement the first choice in the league's draft of college players was to be decided by a coin toss between the two teams with the worst records. And Milwaukee won the coin toss.

That gave the Bucks the negotiating rights to Alcindor, but they were competing against the American Basketball Association's New York Nets. Alcindor chose the Bucks, and on April 2, 1969, he signed the most lucrative contract in sports history for a reported $1.4 million spread over five years.

Alcindor would rather have played in New York. As he

ABC's Wide World of Sports Special

Lew Alcindor's Pro Debut

MILWAUKEE VS DETROIT

Live
2:00PM
abc Saturday 7

It was a game heralded for TV-viewing by ABC.

put it, "If I had had 100 choices of where I wanted to play, 99 of them would have been New York. But I accepted the NBA offer because it was more solid."

Lew was used to two of the three largest cities in the United States, so the prospect of playing in Milwaukee did not appeal to him at first. He almost seemed homesick. But once he blended into the team and became accustomed to his surroundings, the tall rookie became content. Asked about his feeling going into his first game as a pro, he said, "It's completely new to me, and I'm looking forward to giving my best contribution to the team. After that, I'm not looking forward to anything special. I don't want to go into pro ball thinking I'm the greatest. I haven't proven myself in the pros."

Although he is an intense individual on the basketball floor, Alcindor is the casual type off it, as he proved on the day of his biggest game. A little more than an hour before gametime, just before reporting to the arena, he ate a hamburger with many of the trimmings.

"I don't follow any regular routine before a game," he said, "so it doesn't make any difference that we're playing in the afternoon. I just eat when I'm hungry, that's all. And as far as the game itself is concerned, it's the same 48 minutes no matter when you play it."

In the dressing room, coach Larry Costello reminded his players to work the ball to Alcindor in the middle whenever possible. With the aging Wayne Embry at center the previous season, the Bucks had come to rely on outside shooting.

"It's not easy to break a habit," Costello said, "but when you've got a 7-foot center like Lew, you've got to use him. Not many centers in the league are going to stop him in one-on-one situations."

The Bucks' outside shooting was provided by high-scoring guards Jon McGlocklin and Flynn Robinson. To go with

Alcindor in the forecourt were aggressive young Greg Smith and highly-regarded rookie Bob Dandridge.

Detroit, which had finished just ahead of Milwaukee in the 1968–69 standings, was starting the season with a new head coach—Bill ("Butch") van Breda Kolff. The Pistons could count on only part-time service from their top scorer, Dave Bing, and regular forward Happy Hairston was sidelined for the whole game. But there was still 6-11 Walt Bellamy at center, Terry Dischinger and McCoy McLemore at forwards and solid backcourt strength with Eddie Miles, Butch Komives and Jimmy Walker.

The Bucks took the floor 25 minutes before gametime and Alcindor's appearance brought a roar from the crowd. The million-dollar rookie got another big cheer when he put in his first stuff shot of the warmup period, and still another each time he repeated the maneuver that had been outlawed his last two seasons in college.

When the Bucks were introduced individually, it was Alcindor who received the greatest applause. Finally, the players lined up at midcourt and Alcindor squared off to jump against the veteran Bellamy. To make a tense moment more so, the tipoff had to be held up until one of ABC's cameras was removed from the floor.

"Get ABC out of there," yelled one disgruntled fan.

Alcindor officially began his pro career by winning the tip from Bellamy, and in just 18 seconds he had his first pro field goal. On a set play, he took a pass in the pivot, made a move to his left and sank a turn-around jump shut from 12 feet out. The crowd roared its approval, and Alcindor and the Bucks were on their way.

Three and a half minutes later, with the score 10–9 Milwaukee, Alcindor put in two layups in quick succession. Twice in the ensuing 4 minutes, the Pistons forged ahead, and

He would be on the bench only during time-outs.

JOHN BIEVER

each time Alcindor retrieved the lead for Milwaukee with a hook shot.

Did somebody say the hook shot was dead? It may have been almost nonexistent in recent years, but Alcindor has brought it back, and he can shoot it equally well with either hand.

Before the first quarter was over, Alcindor had sunk two free throws and another turn-around shot. The Bucks led at the quarter, 35–30, and Alcindor had 14 of their 35 points.

The big fellow's point production fell off to 5 in the second period when Detroit replaced Bellamy with the more mobile Otto Moore, but Lew was just as busy and just as much the crowd-pleaser.

It was in this quarter that Alcindor made his most spectacular move of the day. He swept across the court to his left and put in a left-handed "suspension" hook shot, holding the ball on his fingertips and hanging in midair for what seemed seconds before releasing the ball. The shot was disallowed, however, because Alcindor was charged with an offensive foul.

Alcindor had just brought the Bucks from behind for the third time with another short jump shot—and this would have been the fourth time—if he hadn't fouled. As it was, the Bucks got the ball back immediately and Guy Rodgers scored from the corner to give them a 51–50 lead.

The Bucks allowed the invaders to climb into a 53–53 tie, but Alcindor broke the deadlock with a free throw and Milwaukee went on to a 60–53 lead at the intermission.

At halftime of his first official pro game, Alcindor had 19 points, 6 rebounds and 2 assists. And this being an occasion to showcase the remarkable rookie to the nation, he had more to do between halves than just listen to coach Costello. He

9

was Jack Twyman's second halftime guest on the ABC telecast, following NBA commissioner Walter Kennedy.

"I'm disappointed in my shooting," Alcindor said in the interview. "I took some bad shots, and I missed some good ones."

Alcindor had been slightly below par in marksmanship with his eight baskets in seventeen attempts. That figured out to a 47.1 per cent average, compared with a phenomenal collegiate three-year mark of 63.9 per cent. Even so, he had lived up to everything that had been said about him, perhaps more.

Nineteen seconds after the second half began, Alcindor scored on another hook shot. Two minutes later he sank still another of the turn-around shots that he makes look so easy, and then he drew *ohs* and *ahs* from the crowd when he blocked a shot by McLemore, only to be called for goaltending.

Late in the third quarter, the big guy was charged with goaltending of another variety—offensive. He was ruled to have touched the ball when it was on the rim after being shot by teammate Bob Dandridge, so a field goal was nullified.

Alcindor didn't score again in that period—he again settled for five points—but his colleagues kept the points coming and the Bucks carried a 91–81 advantage into the final 12 minutes.

The Milwaukee margin continued to mount in the early minutes of the fourth quarter, and with 8:34 to play, Alcindor sent the Bucks over the 100 mark by putting in a rebound. He added a layup on a pass from Robinson, then returned the favor by throwing a floor-length pass to Robinson, who caught the ball like an end and scored on a layup.

A free throw with 6:35 left was to finish Alcindor's scoring for the day, but it was not his last contribution. He assisted on

10

goals by Greg Smith and Fred Crawford, blocked one Detroit shot legally and was called for goaltending again when he knocked down another.

The Bucks left the court with an impressive 119–110 victory, and when the final returns were counted, Alcindor had more than lived up to his billing as the star attraction. He had played the full 48 minutes and scored 29 points, hauled in 12 rebounds, 6 assists, blocked three shots (plus the two on which he was called for goaltending), intercepted three passes and intimidated Detroit players who ventured near the basket. He had sunk 12 field goals in 27 tries, plus 5 of 8 foul shots.

Besides setting up six baskets with his passing, Alcindor had paved the way for many others by rebounding and getting the ball downcourt for fast breaks. He had even displayed his agility by dribbling halfway down the floor like a 6-foot guard after one of his interceptions.

It was the type of debut that most athletes only dream about. Afterward, Twyman—himself a former All-Pro with the Cincinnati Royals—led the cheering for the twenty-two-year-old New Yorker.

"This could be the start of big things in Milwaukee," said Twyman. "Alcindor plays like Bill Russell [who had led the Boston Celtics to eleven titles in thirteen years], and he's a better shooter. But beyond his shooting, I was impressed with the way he made the team move. His ability to hit the open man is amazing. He's a complete ballplayer, and a very unselfish ballplayer. His teammates know that if they get open they'll get the ball. He has transformed this club into a confident bunch that is ready to challenge anybody."

Piston coach van Breda Kolff was somewhat reserved in his praise, saying, "He ought to be able to see the open man, the way he's looking down on everybody out there. Sure, he passes

In the pros there's no law against dunking.   UPI

the ball well. He's supposed to. He's got good moves, but remember, it's that much easier for him with his size. He's got a lot of advantages."

Alcindor proved himself something of a perfectionist when he said after his debut, "I didn't care too much for my play. I made a lot of mistakes."

But mistakes or no mistakes, the overwhelming consensus was that Alcindor would be basketball's next superstar—and soon. Even the usually conservative coach Costello said, "I believe that without any question. He's got all the skills, all the talents and, most of all, a great attitude. He can't miss being a superstar."

The roughness of pro basketball notwithstanding, Alcindor said he already liked it better than the college brand. He noted that there were no zone defenses to crimp his activity around the basket, and no rule to prevent him from stuffing.

"Besides," he said, "there's no studying, and the pay is better."

2

BRADLEY VS. CAZ

Leonard Koppett

•

•

It was right after Christmas, but for the basketball fans of
New York the most delectable present was still to be un-
wrapped: the eyeball-to-eyeball confrontation (a little more
than 6 feet above floor level) between the already legendary
Bill Bradley of Princeton and the already dazzling Cazzie Russell of Michigan.

This was December, the last few days of the year 1964,
and the place was Madison Square Garden on Eighth Avenue
and Forty-ninth Street in Manhattan—the "real" Madison
Square Garden to anyone over forty, the quickly forgotten
piece of ancient history to today's younger set.

The present Garden, where Bradley and Russell now play

17

*Bill Bradley has the ball and alongside is his Michigan
rival, Cazzie Russell.*   UPI

as New York Knickerbockers, is a huge indoor bowl set atop Penn Station, proudly free of structural posts, vast, clean, color-engineered with upholstered seats, antiseptically air-conditioned. But the old Garden was a rectangle, twice as long as it was wide, with the side balcony and mezzanine virtually hanging over the side of the court and the tops of the end arena and balcony receding into the smoky distance. It had two things the present Garden does not: intimacy and the untransferable tradition that this was the building in which big-time basketball was born and raised.

It was here that Ned Irish's college doubleheaders of the mid-1930s created intersectional play and the profit potential. It was here that, in 1938, the first major tournament (the National Invitation) took root. It was here that sellout after sellout made the advent of modern professional basketball inevitable. And it was here, in the winter of 1950–51, that the first great scandals blew the college basketball structure to bits.

At that time, in an atmosphere of reconstruction in which college administrations tried to take greater control of basketball promotion, the Eastern College Athletic Conference Holiday Basketball Festival was invented. It would take place during the Christmas holidays instead of at the end of the season, and several "host" teams from the ECAC would be joined by two or three invitees from other sections.

Now, by 1964, the scandals had been lived down and the Festival had been built up as the major midseason tournament of the college schedule. This particular Festival would be the most glamorous and draw the biggest crowds yet; but its crux was the possibility that Bradley and Russell might bring their teams to face each other in the semifinal round.

No promoter could have invented a matchup with more intriguing aspects. Here was Princeton, epitome of the Ivy

18

League, the top of the social scale and—inevitably—downgraded as "soft" for precisely those reasons. And here was Michigan, with a rich but quite different social tradition of its own, a state university representing avowed worship of athletic prowess as a mainstay of the Big Ten, but also counted among the intellectual leaders of these immense Midwestern mass-education institutions.

Nor could the individual leaders, Bradley and Russell, have been more perfectly cast. Here was Bradley, slim at 6-5, son of a banker, a St. Louis suburbanite, white, a Rhodes Scholar headed for Oxford, a victorious participant in the 1964 Olympics at Tokyo, the most favored of individuals—yet one who, by endless hard work, motivated by a sort of perfectionism, had turned himself into an All-American athlete with a burning competitive spirit. It was obvious to all that Princeton, whatever the virtues of coach Bill van Breda Kolff and the other players, would compete nationally only because of Bradley's special skills.

And Russell? The same height but much more heavily muscled and stronger; black, from Chicago, rising from an ordinarily hopeless life situation in the way many thousands had before him, by making his athletic ability open doors to education and opportunity. And in the context of Michigan, Cazzie—no matter how clearly he was the best basketball player they had, and no matter how much he contributed to victory—was not the unique and indispensable element making victory thinkable. Michigan had always been and would always be loaded with athletic talent, and Cazzie's present squad had height, speed, strength and competitive experience that Ivy Leaguers lacked.

And so, in anticipation, basketball fans could conjure in their minds some classical confrontations: brains vs. brawn (not in the sense that Michigan's brawn lacked brains, but

19

that Princeton's brains certainly lacked brawn); the elite against the commoners—on the ground that commoners usually command; East vs. Midwest; Ivy League vs. Big Ten. Not, strangely enough, black vs. white so much in the context of that particular time.

The preliminaries broke perfectly, too. In the first round, Michigan crushed Manhattan, 90–77, and displayed its heralded virtues. Cazzie scored 36 points. "Most of Russell's points were scored fairly close to the basket," said *The New York Times* the next morning, "on drives, rebounds, jump shots within 10 feet. But he never stopped, and his body, as with most great offensive players, seemed to move in sections."

It was striking that Cazzie, at 6-5 and strong, could play backcourt for Michigan because Bill Bunting, Oliver Darden and Larry Tregoning gave the team so much size and power up front.

Bradley, on the other hand, was a cornerman for Princeton, and key rebounder as well as scorer, and he was watched more carefully and skeptically in Princeton's first-round game against Syracuse. Princeton was a decided underdog (automatically, as Ivy League) and Syracuse had, among other assets, a young backcourtman named Dave Bing.

But Bradley made his impression in the opening minutes. Syracuse used a four-man zone against him, with the fifth man concentrating entirely on Bradley. He was hooked, held, shoved and harassed at every step, with or without the ball— but every time he was hit he hit back, and never lost his concentration. He scored 23 points in the first half, which ended with Princeton leading 45–44, and had 36 when he fouled out with 3 minutes to play and Princeton ahead by 13. It ended 79–69 (with, incidentally, 28 points for Bing).

The basketball community, having put him under a microscope, was impressed. Carl Braun, a former Knick star and coach then functioning as a scout, summed up what dozens of other observers put in almost identical words: "Bradley has a fabulous shooting touch, all the skills, he belts back and he has terrific court sense. Russell has terrific energy, quick and deceptive moves, good ballhandling and good passing, although he's not too much on defense."

On the day between the first and semifinal rounds, no other topic of conversation was possible. At an ECAC luncheon for coaches and press, van Breda Kolff got up. Michigan coach Dave Strack was tied up at some other affair, so Butch addressed his remarks to Jim Skala, Michigan's assistant coach. "Whaddaya say we just play them one-on-one and take the other four off the floor?" said Butch, smiling. It was obviously a self-serving declaration, since Princeton would hardly suggest having its other four play Michigan's other four.

A famous columnist (Milton Gross of the New York *Post*) asked Skala, "Will you relay that request to the coach?"

Said Skala to Gross, "I'm sure *you* will."

Said van Breda Kolff about Skala, "That boy will be a head coach real soon."

"Actually," van Breda Kolff continued, "if we could get the officials in on it, and they'd let the boys have 10 personal fouls each, it would be pretty interesting."

Butch had the right idea in several ways, as the pretty interesting real game would soon show.

That old building, with its deep well and overhanging sides, created greater noise impact on the players and others at floor level than the new one does, even if the actual decibel count is higher in the new one. The degree of concentration, of everything focusing down on the combat zone, was greater there. And when it was jammed again to its capacity of 18,-499 on December 30, 1964, the absolutely joyful tension

21

and excitement reached a peak seldom equalled anywhere.

Michigan's plans were obvious and direct: sweep the boards and run Princeton off the court; it wouldn't really matter much what Bradley scored individually. Princeton's task was also simply stated, but very few believed it could be carried out: check Michigan's fast break, minimize its height by taking only the surest shots and let Bradley operate with his incredible, off-balance jump shots.

In the first half, the Tigers got back on defense so quickly that Michigan's fast break went nowhere. And when a shot went up, Princeton boxed out so well that Michigan didn't get a second try. On offense, with Chris Chimera and Gary Walters the main ballhandlers, they went to Bradley again and again, and he hit—and when covered he fed a teammate.

By halftime there was no question at all who was winning the duel: Bradley.

Bradley had 23 points. Cazzie, guarded by Don Rodenbach, had 8. Bradley, guarding Darden, had held him to 1 point. And Princeton was leading, 39–37. Furthermore, Michigan had been losing its poise against the unexpected resistance from the "soft" Ivy Leaguers. It developed no pattern to compensate for the checked fast break, and it was being out-hustled again and again in the unexpected situations that mark basketball reality. Robby Brown, the tall Princeton center, and Bob Haarlow and Rodenbach were holding their own against the more celebrated Michigan frontcourt—but everything, of course, revolved around Bradley.

But it would probably be different in the second half. Michigan would get over its shock at Princeton's stubbornness. Physical ability would tell. Princeton would inevitably wilt. The ball would start taking different bounces. Cazzie would find the range, adjustments would be made, Bradley had to miss a few, form would assert itself.

Now Cazzie drives in for a layup; Bradley's on the far right.   UPI

After the intermission, Bradley—and Princeton—played better. He kept hitting. Michigan remained disorganized. Princeton pulled ahead. And now a new dimension of Bradley's game appeared. When Michigan went into a full-court press, it was Bradley who brought the ball up. When a certain amount of killing the clock had to be done, Bradley did it. As the Princeton lead mounted and the clock ticked away, Bradley conducted a freeze for more than 1½ minutes. With about 4 minutes to play, Princeton had a 13-point lead. The upset was about to happen. But everything has its price, and the kind of effort Bradley was making had a standard price: fatigue—and fouls.

Oliver Darden drove for the basket. A tired Bill Bradley reached. A whistle blew. Foul—fifth foul. Bradley, who had scored 41 points, was out of the game.

The ovation he got as he left the floor could not be surpassed for sincerity. This was not, essentially, "rooting interest" applause, but "appreciation" applause. This crowd was heavily populated with connoisseurs of the basketball art. It was cheering performance, and the man capable of producing it, quite apart from winning and losing—and, of course, such a performance meant winning.

But there were still nearly 4 minutes to play. And Cazzie Russell was still on the floor. Bradley, after all, had been painted (for three years now) as the all-perfect all-everything. But Cazzie (still a junior) had been most eye-catching in a more specific—but no less important respect. He was (the Midwesterners told us) the supreme "clutch" player, the man who made the end-of-the-game baskets, the man who somehow pulled off those last-second victories. Now he would have his chance. There was 3:35 to play, and Princeton led by 14 points, 77–63.

Cazzie got the ball. He scored.

24

He stole a pass, and scored again.

He stole another, and passed to John Thompson (the other backcourtman) for another basket.

Princeton lost the ball again, and Thompson scored again. And then Cazzie hit again.

Only 66 seconds had elapsed, but now Princeton's lead was only 77–73.

Michigan kept up the pressure, Princeton strove desperately to hold on to the ball. Michigan scored again. Michigan then fouled and Princeton made it 78–75.

Cazzie Russell took off for the basket. He was hit. He shot. The ball went in. He went to the foul line and tossed it in again. A three-pointer—78–78.

Princeton shot and missed. Michigan got possession. This would be the last shot—and not much question about who would take it. This is where Cazzie Russell lived, the reputation said—in the closing seconds taking the last shot needed to win.

Three seconds left on the clock. Cazzie jumps, Cazzie lets go, ball goes through—2 points, scramble, hysteria, buzzer, game over.

Michigan, 80; Princeton, 78.

Bradley won the battle. Michigan won the war.

Life always has sequels, but this is not the place for them. (Michigan didn't even win this tournament, being upset by St. John's in the final for one of coach Joe Lapchick's greatest triumphs.) The season went on, with all sorts of additional heroics by both Bradley and Russell. Bradley then went to England to study; Cazzie played another All-American season, then was drafted by the Knicks. He got a three-year $200,000 deal for signing and helped redesign the whole economic structure of pro basketball. A year later, Bradley came back and made a four-year, half-million-dollar deal, and

25

they became Knick teammates. (By then, the new Garden was built and its opening both dictated and justified such expenditures.)

Neither Bradley nor Cazzie has become, so far at least, anywhere as dominant among the pros. Some reasons for this are obvious: each is that "in-between" size, not perfectly suited to either backcourt or frontcourt in the pro world. And Bradley had the long layoff and Russell injuries. Also, a hundred other things.

But as college players, they were unsurpassed in attractiveness, and those who saw them play in that memorable game at the old Garden retain a spectator's experience that's worth far more than whatever that one ticket cost.

And nothing either ever does as a pro, however successful, will diminish that occasion.

3

WILT AND ELG

Sandy Padwe

•

•

The light cut through the early winter darkness, illuminating the huge marquee with the red letters outside Convention Hall in West Philadelphia. It was shortly before 7 P.M., starting time for the first game of the doubleheader between the Detroit Pistons and Chicago Packers. The Philadelphia Warriors and Los Angeles Lakers would meet in the second game.

It was a quiet, easy evening for the men sitting behind the ticket windows in the outer lobby. There would be no sellout tonight. In fact, the crowd looked as if it might be below 5,000. It was Friday, December 8, 1961, and Christmas

29

Another basket for Philadelphia's Wilt Chamberlain as Los Angeles' Jerry West (44), Ray Felix and Elgin Baylor (22) watch it happen.   WIDE WORLD PHOTOS

shopping, not professional basketball, occupied the minds of many Philadelphians.

Nine Pistons—led by Walter Dukes with 21 points—scored in double figures as Detroit had an easy time with the hapless Packers, 133–107, in the drab opener. It was not a very lively contest and the crowd of 4,022 hoped that the second game might be a bit more exciting.

The Lakers had come to town safely atop the Western Division of the National Basketball Association, having won 19 of their first 26 games. The Warriors were struggling, despite the presence of 7-1 Wilt Chamberlain at center. Wilt certainly scored more than his share of points, but even so the Warriors were having trouble gaining on the Boston Celtics, who were, even at this early point in the pennant race, far ahead in the Eastern Division.

The game would be matching three of the sport's finest performers—Chamberlain of the Warriors against Elgin Baylor and Jerry West of the Lakers. Baylor, among many other feats, held the record for most points in a single game in the NBA with 71. He set that record November 15, 1960, in Madison Square Garden against the New York Knickerbockers. Baylor was from Washington, D.C., and Seattle University. West had played for Laker coach Fred Schaus as an undergraduate at West Virginia University.

The gangling Chamberlain had been a schoolboy star in Philadelphia, at Overbrook High School, about a fifteen-minute ride from Convention Hall. From there he had gone to the University of Kansas and then to the Harlem Globetrotters before joining Eddie Gottlieb's Philadelphia Warriors.

From the moment Chamberlain entered the NBA for the 1959–60 season, every expert in the game predicted instant fame and stardom and a clean sweep of the record book. Wilt averaged 37.6 points per game his rookie year and followed that up with a 38.4 mark his second season. Now, in his third year, he was off to his quickest start.

The 6-5 Baylor, whose slippery fakes and fantastic body control enabled him to outmaneuver many taller forwards, had entered the league one year before Chamberlain. He averaged 24.9, 29.6 and 34.8 in his first three seasons. Whenever these two players met head-on, the fans were assured of some excitement. On this particular evening, the Warriors started quickly. With Chamberlain scoring 13 points, the Warriors jumped to a 34–25 lead. At the end of the first quarter, Baylor had scored 12.

The Warriors held the same 9-point lead at halftime, and Wilt had tallied 28 points to 16 for Baylor. In the third period, Baylor hit from every angle and threw in 16 points, and when the buzzer sounded to end the period the Lakers had a 2-point lead.

As the final period began, the fans knew that Baylor and Chamberlain were in a scoring duel—with Chamberlain ahead 38 to 32.

Sid Borgia and Norm Drucker were the NBA officials assigned to the game and they were under pretty strong bombardment from Warrior coach Frank McGuire, who was charging that the Lakers were using an illegal zone to defense Chamberlain. But the officials did not agree with the Warrior coach and the game proceeded. With 4 minutes remaining, the Warriors led, 105–95, and some were starting for the exits. Then four baskets by Baylor and one each by Frank Selvy and Rudy LaRusso tied the score at 107. It was an arching basket by Baylor, driving around the Warriors' Tom Meschery, that tied the score at 109 at the end of regulation play.

At this stage, Chamberlain had scored 53 points and Baylor 47. So now the fans settled back for the 5-minute overtime that would decide the well-played but grueling game. Chamberlain was the more dominant figure in the overtime, scoring 9 points to 3 for Baylor. But at the buzzer, Al Attles, the Warriors' tough little guard, scored on a layup to apparently win the game, 123–121. The officials, however, said that Attles had released the ball after the buzzer sounded.

So the first overtime ended with a deadlock at 121, again the tying basket having come on a Baylor jump shot. In the second overtime, the drama was packed into the final minute of play.

Sub forward Ed Conlin hit 2 free throws for the Warriors to give them a 133–132 lead with 18 seconds left on the clock. Baylor drove for the basket, stopped 8 feet out and went up with a jumper. Chamberlain's huge arm knocked the ball loose. Elgin and Wilt scrambled for it. A whistle blew. Players froze. Fans froze.

Finally, Borgia pointed to Chamberlain and gave the sign for pushing. Baylor had two chances to win the game. He missed his first shot and made the second for a tie at 133 as the second overtime ended. By now, Chamberlain had scored 68 points and Baylor 59 and it appeared that Wilt was on his way to a record, but it would be a record with an asterisk beside it because Baylor's 71 points had been scored in 48 minutes of regulation play.

The second overtime produced an NBA oddity that could have forced a protest ruling from league headquarters. Schaus, the Laker coach, had protested at one point during the overtime that his team had been short-changed on the free-throw line. Officials and reporters checked and found that the Laker coach was correct. The rule was that in any period, the second personal against a team in the final 2 minutes allows the team that is fouled an extra shot. With 1:46 left, Baylor had shot one free throw. And Tom Hawkins made another foul shot with 46 seconds left, but didn't get the second one. With 41 seconds remaining, and time out, Schaus protested about Hawkins' trip to the foul line. Borgia upheld the protest and allowed Hawkins an extra free throw, which he missed. However, Baylor never shot a second free throw.

So as the third overtime period began, there was pandemonium in Convention Hall, and Chamberlain was nearing the single-game scoring mark.

Chamberlain finally broke the record with 3:10 remaining in the third overtime when he took a high pass from Tom Gola and turned right to drop it in. He was fouled on the play by Hawkins and made the free throw. The 3-point play gave the Warriors a 141–138 edge and brought the fans to their feet.

When things had grown a bit calmer and the teams settled down, West became the key figure in the game. A basket by Jerry gave the Lakers a 142–141 edge, then two free throws by Meschery put the Warriors back on top, 145–144, with 1:15 left.

Then West, Hawkins and finally Howie Joliff, a 6-7 forward who had to guard Chamberlain when Jim Krebs, Ray Felix and LaRusso fouled out, scored baskets and the Lakers went on to win, 151–147, despite a final output by Chamberlain of 78. Baylor finished with 63 and West 32.

By periods, the breakdown between Chamberlain and Baylor read like this: Chamberlain, 13-15-10-15-9-6-10—78. Baylor, 12-4-16-15-3-9-4—63.

The Warriors' dressing room, despite the record-shattering performance by Chamberlain, was as gloomy as if the world championship had been lost. Chamberlain could not even smile about the record.

"Record?" he said, sadly. "What record? All I was interested in was winning this game."

Finally, after a little prodding by reporters, Wilt relaxed a bit. "Losing a game like that takes all the kick out of the record," he said as he took huge gulps from a half-gallon container of milk. "We should have won the game. They just got too many easy rebounds. Every time it seemed like the ball was coming off right in their hands.

"No, I didn't know how many points I had or when I broke the record. I was busy trying to win the game. Seventy-eight points down the drain."

Chamberlain was asked if the Lakers had employed a box-and-one zone. "You can see as well as anyone, can't you?" Chamberlain snarled at reporters.

Chamberlain took 62 shots in the game to break another record, this one belonging to ex-Warrior Joe Fulks. Wilt's 31 field goals also broke Baylor's record of 28, set on the night he established the old record. And from the free-throw line the big guy hit on 16 out of 31. Baylor made 23 of 55 shots during the triple-overtime and converted 17 of 24 free throws.

In the Laker dressing room there was laughter and joking. Someone asked Baylor if he cared that Chamberlain had broken his record in overtime. Baylor smiled and said, "Wilt has the record, period. He deserves it after the game he played tonight. But we won the ballgame, and I wouldn't trade that for any record. We've got 20 wins now and that's the only record I'm interested in."

4

BIG O
AND BIG SPOON

Ira Berkow

•

It seemed like a funny time to stop a game. Was there an injury? A foul-up at the scorer's table? Or had a player suggested that a referee visit an optometrist?

The buzzer groaned, the game halted and the players— like windup toys that had run out—stopped and looked around with pinched eyebrows.

The suspense was soon lifted. "Oscar Robertson," explained the public-address announcer at Cincinnati Gardens, "has just made his 6,950th career assist, more than anyone in the history of the National Basketball Association. The record was held by Bob Cousy."

Oscar, the Big O, stood near midcourt. His white shorts

"Robertson has the supreme confidence that he can do anything any time."   MALCOLM W. EMMONS

appeared, as always, a bit droopy. His long arms hung at his sides. His forehead was wrinkled and he seemed gently embarrassed as the players around him—his Royal teammates and the Phoenix Suns, the reporters at courtside and the crowd of 3,933 (about one-third of capacity)—applauded. Referee Ed Rush walked over to Robertson and stuck the game ball in his chest. Now the fans stood, still applauding and cheering.

In the front row across from the scorer's table, three gals stood, too. From left to right they were: Shana Robertson, soon to be seven years old, in yellow knit dress, yellow bows in pigtails and blue tights; Tia Robertson, age five, in red knit dress and red bow in ponytail; and their mother, Yvonne, green and gray knit dress and in the family way. They clapped for their breadwinner. The two younger ladies tired, sat down again—swinging feet that did not touch the floor—and returned to their popcorn. ("The girls weren't too excited about the honor," said Mrs. Robertson later. "In fact, they wanted the game to hurry and continue. I'm sure they don't understand the significance of the record. But they do love to clap for baskets. They used to cheer for every basket—even for the other team's. But they're more discriminating now.")

The pass that broke the career record could hardly have come at a more inauspicious time. It was near the end of the first quarter and the crowd had not yet been stirred. The thump of bouncing ball, the squeak of sneakers, the grunts of players was distinct. The teams were both low in the standings. The Royals were in fifth place in the Eastern Division, but still had some hope of catching the fourth-place Boston Celtics and making the playoffs; the Suns, a first-year expansion team, were deep in last place in the West. It was February 16, 1969, and the long NBA season—with its thousands of miles of travel and sleeping in beds too short or too camel-backed or too swayed, and the foot blisters, the strained calf muscles, the mental enervation—had a little over a month left. And all this showed in the players' performance this late afternoon. The Royals, especially, appeared stick-stiff. They had played a tough game in Chicago the night before, beating the Bulls, 111–101. Their plane had not arrived back in Cincinnati until 3:30 A.M. Robertson got to bed about an hour later. He had been suffering with a thigh injury and needed all the rest he could get.

He awoke around noon, ate, lolled around the house listening to rock-and-roll and blues albums and playing with his daughters, then he departed for the game. His family followed sometime later. There was no thought of records.

"Someone had mentioned to me a few days before that I was getting close to Cousy's record," said Robertson later. "But I forgot about it."

Going into this NBA season, his ninth, Robertson had 6,401 career assists (an assist is a pass that leads directly to a field goal). It had taken Cousy 13 seasons—from 1950–51 to 1962–63—to feed off for 6,949 baskets with the Celtics. After the Chicago game, Robertson was only three short of breaking Cousy's record.

Four minutes into the first quarter of the Phoenix game, Robertson drove, pulling two men on him, then flipped to Fred Hetzel under the basket for 2 points. A few minutes later Robertson passed to Jerry Lucas, cutting under the basket, for the feed that tied the record. But there was no announcement. Andy Cox, Royals' publicity director, was waiting for the record-breaker. He was certain it would come this day. Robertson's career assists average was over 10 a game, and now he was again leading the league with a 9.4 average. What fool would bet that Robertson would not get at least three assists in this game? Certainly not Andy Cox. He had

39

been preparing for this moment for several weeks and had tried to obtain a giant spoon to present to Robertson when he broke the record. The spoon was to symbolize "The Great Feeder." But there was a mix-up with the manufacturer and the spoon would not be ready for another week or so. Cox was disheartened.

The game, though close in score, was as exciting as watching grass grow. Near the end of the first quarter the Royals were leading, 23–21. Jerry Lucas pulled down a defensive rebound and passed to Oscar on the right side. Robertson dribbled up to the half-court line where he was stopped by two defenders, Dick Snyder and Gale Goodrich. Through a windmill of arms, Robertson slipped a 20-foot pass to Tom Van Arsdale, open at the top of the key. Oscar likes playing with Van Arsdale because Tom is always in motion. It opens many more offensive patterns for Oscar, who as the Royals' top playmaker and scorer—handles the ball about 90 per cent of the time. "It helps when you have someone like Tom running downcourt that way," says Robertson. The pass was deft enough to get by the Phoenix defenders, swift enough to give Van Arsdale time before another defender could come up to get him, soft enough for Van Arsdale to handle easily and chest-high for the ultimate in shooting convenience. Van Arsdale hit the 15-foot jump shot. It came with 1:41 left in the first quarter. The record was broken, the buzzer sounded.

When Robertson came to the Royals in the fall of 1960, he was known primarily as a shooter. He had just ended an unparalleled college career at the University of Cincinnati. He had led the nation in scoring in each of his three varsity seasons. No one had ever done that before.

Soon he was scoring 30 points a game and leading even Wilt Chamberlain—who is some 9 inches taller than the 6-5 Robertson—in the NBA scoring race.

Referee Ed Rush gave Oscar the ball after he broke Bob Cousy's record. UPI

"Oscar can't miss being one of the greatest players ever," said Jack Twyman, the Royals' standout shooting forward, midway through the 1960–61 season. "He's a great student of the game, along with having tremendous natural ability. He has taken over as a leader and he makes us go. He's to us what Bob Cousy is to the Celtics. Everybody knows he's a great shot, but few know he can pass with Cousy."

Dick McGuire, then the Detroit Pistons' coach and formerly an outstanding NBA playmaker, went further: "Oscar is better than Cousy ever was; Oscar is the finest player in basketball."

And Cousy himself added, "Robertson is the best of his kind ever to come into the league."

Cousy, in his first two seasons (1950–51 and 1951–52), averaged 4.9 and 6.7 assists per game. Andy Phillips of the Philadelphia Warriors had led the league then with marks of 6.3 and 7.2. Then from 1952–53 until Robertson came into the league eight seasons later, Cousy was the NBA's leading playmaker.

In Robertson's first year, 1960–61, he broke Cousy's dominance in that department. Robertson averaged 9.7 assists per game, Cousy 7.8.

Besides Robertson needing four fewer seasons than Cousy to reach the assists figure, other statistical passing comparisons are interesting: Cousy's highest assists average was 9.5, the year before Robertson entered the league. Robertson's highest, an NBA record, was 11.5 in 1964–65; his lowest was 9.5. The most assists Cousy ever had in one season was 715. Only once has Oscar been below that figure, and that was his rookie year; his highest total established a league record, 899 in 1961–62.

"Cousy was a great passer, no question about that," said Jack McMahon, who coached the Royals for several years and was also a fine backcourtman in the NBA. "But Bob was flashy, and sometimes he looked better than he actually was. He would drive up the middle and go into the air, then pass behind his back. It would have been better had he stopped at the free-throw line and passed for a clear shot. Oscar, meanwhile, never commits himself until absolutely necessary. He almost always has both feet on the ground."

Van Arsdale added, "Oscar does nothing fancy with his passing. Everything is basic. Just the fundamentals. But he takes advantage of every little wrong move of the opposition. He throws passes I would never dream of throwing. Robertson has the supreme confidence that he can do anything anytime."

"I feel very strongly about the value of passing," said Robertson. "I may score 40 or 50 points, but I consider it a bad night if I don't have at least 10 assists as well." He added that he took a great deal of pride in leading the NBA in assists five times in his first six seasons.

Robertson's passing excellence and records are due to a variety of reasons. First is his natural ability, his quick reflexes, his superior peripheral vision, his long hours of concentration and practice. "But most of all," he says, "a passer has to be unselfish."

Another important factor is Robertson's scoring ability, which has increased his passing effectiveness. Often double- and triple-teamed, he must of necessity look for a cutting teammate. "If you double-team Oscar for a second," said Tom Heinsohn, the former Celtic star who is now the Boston coach, "you gamble. That calls for a pass, and he'll pass it."

In the locker room after his record-breaking game against the Suns, Robertson sat in a corner, undressing slowly. The Royals had lost, 125–113, and dropped further behind the Celtics, their chances of making the playoffs slimmer.

A reporter asked Robertson how he felt when presented with the game ball in the first quarter.

"Tired," he said, unsmiling. "It gave me a chance to rest."

Any special thrill?

"No," he said, unlacing his basketball shoes. "If we had won the game, or if we were higher in the standings, then maybe I would have gotten a little excited about it. But my job is to play the game as best I can, to make a worthwhile contribution to the team. Sure, I'm proud of the achievement. But records are made to be broken. And someone will come along to break this one."

From anyone else the answer might have been humble at best, a cliché at worst. From Robertson, a withdrawn man, a driven basketball player, it emerged as a pristine statement of fact.

Now, outside the locker room, only a few people remained. At courtside, there sounded the click of typewriters as reporters wrote against deadlines. A few players' wives were seated in a small cluster, talking softly.

On the court, several children ran around the basket tossing up paper wads and squealing. Shana and Tia Robertson were among them, jumping and throwing and missing every time. Tia ran to her mother, grabbed a fistful of popcorn from yet another box and ran back to try again. Like their father, Shana and Tia had no thoughts of records either.

5

THE LIVING-ROOM BOUNCE

Joseph P. Val

•

•

"Good evening, ladies and gentlemen, this is Bill Allen speaking from Madison Square Garden, where the National Broadcasting Company is about to bring you the *first* televised basketball game. . . ."

This announcement by Bill Allen—whoever *he* was—was made at 8:16 P.M. on February 28, 1940. It capped an historic week for indoor sports on television. In the fast-moving new medium, the practicality of doing outdoor sports had been established nearly a year earlier. Bill Stern became TV's first sports voice on May 17, 1939, when he described a Princeton–Columbia baseball game at Baker Field in New York City. Two weeks later, Sam Taub announced the first

47

Burke Crotty directed the first basketball game on television. NBC

TV fight—Lou Nova–Max Baer—at Yankee Stadium. In the summer of '39 major-league baseball made its television debut with Red Barber's coverage of the Cincinnati Reds–Brooklyn Dodgers doubleheader at Ebbets Field. And football was first televised in the early fall of that year when Waynesburg (Pennsylvania) played at Fordham; pro football, with "Bill Allen" announcing, arrived on the magic box in midseason when the Philadelphia Eagles played the Brooklyn Dodgers at Ebbets Field.

Encouraged by these experiences, W2XBS—NBC's experimental station—decided to televise indoor sports in the last week of February 1940. The first TV track meet (National AAU Championships) was shown on February 24 from Madison Square Garden, and on the next night—and from the same arena—came the first TV hockey game—New York Rangers–Montreal Canadiens.

Then came basketball's inaugural, pairing Pitt–Fordham in the opener and NYU–Georgetown in the nightcap. The twin bill provided another new challenge for Burke Crotty, a young dynamo from the National Broadcasting Company out of the NBC press department who was directing all the sports shows.

"Everything we did was a *first,* good or bad," Crotty would recall three decades later. "One of the early ventures put me in a ticklish spot. I was fired the day after I televised the *first* wrestling match from a neighborhood club. 'Not sufficiently dignified,' was one executive's snobbish verdict. But the firing didn't stick."

There were at the time an estimated 300 TV receivers, all in the New York area. In the main they were donated to newspaper editors and critics and to advertising executives. A few receivers were purchased at $660 each by tavern owners, and they, of course, drew most of the viewers.

48

In the bars the lookers had to form a tight huddle because those bulky models had no giant screen. The lid of the 4-foot-high cabinetlike sets had to be raised and propped at an angle to get the picture. The underside of the lid had a mirror that reflected the image from the glass surface of the inside top of the cabinet.

How much basketball fans were crowded around sets for the opening doubleheader will never be known. But nobody can dispute that there was little notice given the games. The newspapers viewed the newcomer as a rival that would affect daily circulation. Program listings were minimal; some publishers insisted that the station should pay advertising rates if it wished to see its schedule in print. NBC asked viewers to write in for a special printing of listings.

The sports pages of the eleven newspapers in New York made no mention of the basketball experiment with "visual radio" in their advance stories. The three-cent *New York Times* had no daily devotion to TV, although the ten-cent Sunday edition carried the week's events. These didn't require much space, to be sure, since the program schedule of station W2XBS (New York) usually consisted of three or four items, covering perhaps four hours. A regular daily event was *Lowell Thomas and the News,* 6:15 to 7 P.M. Then came variety shows or testing of the various sports attractions.

The new interest in sports made young Burke Crotty an important figure in the embryonic world of the picture tube. He had a veritable stable of announcing talent to draw from at NBC, yet he came up with an unknown, the one called "Bill Allen," for this *first* in basketball.

"The man came in cold, applied for work and I put him on," explained Crotty. "Bill Stern was our first man on TV, on Columbia baseball, and later on the Garden six-day bike race, which he did with Willie Ratner, the writer. But Stern was too busy with radio. So I was looking for a man."

Crotty's "Bill Allen," was, in fact, Allen William "Skip" Walz, one of New York City's great amateur athletes in the 1930s. Captain of NYU football, heavyweight boxer, yachtsman, oarsman (he would later coach crew at Wisconsin and Yale), Walz had had some public-address experience with Manhattan College football and with baseball at Ebbets Field. Why the name "Bill Allen"? Walz explained, "It seemed to roll off the tongue better."

Crotty's instructions to Walz were to let the picture do the work, with a minimum of talk from the announcer. Earlier in that "indoor-sports TV week," Crotty had determined that the position of his huge 90-pound orthicon camera in Section 11, mezzanine, did not facilitate the best picture. So they moved it to Cage "F" for basketball. The TV broadcasts were made without the use of auxiliary lights. Crotty noted that they utilized "only those lights which are customarily installed for the convenience of the spectators."

Artistically, the New York teams in the doubleheader—Fordham and NYU—did not perform with distinction in basketball's TV debut. If one didn't know better, it might be said they had "mike" fright. Actually, the boys may not have known they were on television. Coaches Ed Kelleher of Fordham and Howard Cann of NYU were not the type to contrive a pep talk. They did not urge their lads to do their all for any "vast hidden audience." Vast it was not. Even the house of 9,657 was only half of capacity.

Fordham lost to Pitt, 57–37, as expected, though the Rams were down only 23–28 at the half. It was in that first half that director Crotty, announcer Allen and assorted technicians—some in a mobile unit on Fiftieth Street outside the Garden—discovered that they'd lost their picture. They were off the

50

air for more than twenty minutes. It was, after all, pioneer TV.

When NYU and Georgetown took the court in the second game—under the all-seeing eye—televiewers and Garden spectators had to be horrified at a dismal performance. Neither Cann's Violets, unbeaten in seventeen games, nor Elmer Ripley's Hoyas could find the hoop. At the intermission the score was an unbelievable 10–7, NYU. And not because of staunch defense but due to miserable shooting.

NYU made a trifling 3 field goals in 30 shots; and Georgetown hit on only 3 of 41. In the second half it was different. NYU bagged 17 of 34 and won easily, 50–27. Its heroes were Red Stevens, Bobby Lewis, Ben Auerbach, Ralph Kaplowitz and Irv Dubinsky.

As for television, director Crotty's official production report stated:

> First basketball broadcast. 8:16 to 10:46 P.M. Bill Allen announcer. Orthicon in cage "F". Excellent picture. Telephone company trouble from approximately 8:26 to 8:50 P.M. At conclusion 1st period of 1st game returned to 5A for intermission sign and network sound while trouble repaired. Back on air about middle of second period of 1st game. Sound mainly PA system and crowd noise except for comment from Allen during breaks.

Neither the players nor the telephone company distinguished themselves that night, but the games made television history as basketball for the first time bounced into a few living rooms and bars. And a fellow named Skip Walz tried to make a new name for himself.

51

6

SURPRISE
FOR THE GLOBETROTTERS

Jack Hewins

•

•

Abe Saperstein made the first mistake of the game. The genial little owner of the fabulous Harlem Globetrotters took one look at the Seattle University basketball team and asked coach Al Brightman, "Is this all you've got?"

Abe certainly was entitled to his opinion, but he should have kept his voice down. Every member of the Seattle Chieftain squad heard what he said, even above the anticipatory growl of the crowd that was bulging the University of Washington Pavilion.

"This is a one-man team," Saperstein had told his Trotters. "All you gotta do is stop the little guy." Scanning the enemy now, Abe wondered if his deck of basketball aces could tell

55

Seattle's Johnny O'Brien goes up with a left hook against the Globetrotters. SEATTLE TIMES which little guy to stop. The starting five had shed their warm-up togs and were grouped around Brightman in their maroon uniforms.

The biggest of the lot, Abe judged with a practiced eye, could be no more than 6 feet 4. A quick check of the boy's number in his program told Abe he was correct, and the boy was Bill Higlin. He guessed Ray Sanford and Jack Doherty, the two forwards, at about 6-2 or 6-3, and then he dropped down to the O'Brien twins, whom he could almost look in the eye when standing on tiptoe. If the program said more than 5-9 it was cheating.

"This is the kid who's leading the colleges of the country in scoring?" Abe asked himself, peering at Johnny O'Brien. At least, he thought it was Johnny, the twin with just a bit of cant in the nose, a souvenir of many collisions.

"I seem to be just elbow-high to everybody," John would say as the team physician patched another break in the Irish proboscis. He stood an exact 5-9 and bragged that he was a quarter-inch taller than brother Ed.

Saperstein moved back to his own cluster of warriors, undoubtedly the most famous basketball team in history. As good as their name, the Harlem Globetrotters had toured the world and were known in every American city and hamlet from coast to coast. Out of habit, Abe appraised the crowd. Fans were sardined into the place so tightly that breathing was a problem. The Pavilion's capacity was 11,500. Tonight the press was guessing the total at 12,500, and the Seattle Fire Department, growing edgy, estimated 13,000 and ordered the doors closed. And Abe's Globetrotters were not to share in a nickel of it. Nor was Seattle U. This was January 21, 1952, and Saperstein's professional stars were playing Brightman's amateur collegians only because the Olympic Games fund was badly in need of money. Howard Hobson, basketball coach at Yale and a member of the Olympic Committee, had cooked up the project along with Saperstein and Royal Brougham, sports editor of the Seattle *Post-Intelligencer*. The National Collegiate Athletic Association surprisingly gave its blessing to this meeting between amateurs and pros. The Trotters and the Chieftains each footed their own bills and the neighboring University of Washington donated its gym free of charge. The fund was to swell that night by more than $9,000.

Looking up at the throaty thousands tiered to the rafters, Saperstein recalled the days when his Trotters toured the back country in cranky cars to play before crowds of half a hundred in leaky-roofed gyms heated by potbellied stoves. Now they were famous as the invincible clowns of basketball with a .936 winning percentage after 3,574 games. They called it "showboatin' "—their pepper games, their hidden-ball tricks, their hilarious arguments with each other and the referees— but the Trotters had a habit of running up a safe margin before they started clowning.

The sound of the whistle pulled Saperstein's thoughts back to the present and he saw the young actress Joan Caulfield— honorary referee for the evening—toss the ball up for the center jump. Higlin and Goose Tatum, one of the Trotters' all-time greats, disregarded the ball and grabbed Miss Caulfield, who squealed in mock fright and ran for the safety of the scorers' table.

"This," she said, "is what you call the fast break."

And that was the end of the showboatin'.

Pop Hagerty, who was teaming with Roy Meyers to referee this rare clash of collegians and professionals, got the ball up at center again and, almost before you could say "Saperstein," Johnny O'Brien was right-hooking it into the basket.

Tatum answered with a left-hand hook for a Trotter basket,

but Johnny O immediately sank a hook from the left and then slipped past the amazed Tatum for a layup that made the count 6–2.

The Trotters now knew which little guy they had to stop. All they needed was someone to tell them how. This particular little guy was so unorthodox he was almost a rule-violation. Wasn't he listed as a guard? Then what was he doing playing the post? That's where the big men played, and the Trotters didn't know that some of the best big men in the Northwest, occasionally a foot taller than Johnny O, had reached and groped and grabbed for the Chieftain wraith while he flitted right and left and filled the ring with points.

The taller O'Brien got to be a post man one night in Bellingham, Washington, when the play was ragged and Western Washington College was threatening to upset the favored Chiefs. At halftime, Brightman, who may have been feigning disgust, stirred his lineup with a strategic spoon that put John at the pivot.

"If you guys don't do something now I have five people who can replace you," growled the coach. They outscored Western, 68–17, in the second half and John had found a new berth.

Goose Tatum, the best of the Trotters, was guarding him now. Tatum reached out to fend off an O'Brien layup, heard Hagerty's whistle and watched Johnny sink two free throws. After that, Johnny O borrowed a Trotter gimmick, catching the ball between his knees and raising his arms in a fake. Tatum went up to block the false shot and when he came down Johnny flipped home an over-the-shoulder 2-pointer.

"Watch that kid—he's travelin'," Goose yelled at Hagerty.

"He sure is, isn't he?" Pop yelled back.

The Trotters called for time and Tatum asked for help.

"What you need," Abe Saperstein told him, "is a net."

Higlin hit a long shot from beyond the key and Sanford

Johnny O attempts a fake on a night he and all Seattle will never forget.
SEATTLE TIMES

picked up points on a jump shot and free throws. Josh Grider looped one home from outside and Ermer Robinson added Trotter tallies on a layup and two free tosses. But mostly the first quarter was a struggle between a pesky O'Brien who came out of a South Amboy, New Jersey, pottery plant and a talented Tatum from the cotton fields of Eldorado, Arkansas.

"Hey, coach," said the impish Doherty as he toweled away the sweat at the quarter break. "Go tell Saperstein he's right —we're all you've got." The score was 22–15 in Seattle's favor and Johnny had 16 of the Chieftain points. Tatum had 10 and an idea. "Hey, Sam," he said to Sam Wheeler, "you take him for a while. We'll change off on him."

Brightman, formerly a professional who had played often against the Trotters, knew the opponents well. "They'll stay with the man-to-man defense," he told his five small people. "You can always get the ball to John. But keep hounding them on those long shots. If you shut off their outside shooting you'll take 'em."

Meyers blew the whistle, grateful for the brief rest. In a huddle before the game with Brightman and Saperstein, it had been decided to follow college rules with 10-minute quarters. They had seemed longer. The thunder of the crowd had dimmed to a muted roar but it swelled again with the return to action. Johnny was at the free-throw line, adding a point for Seattle, but he was having more trouble. He scored only 9 in the second quarter, but the Trotters weren't catching up. They were missing Marques Haynes, nearly as great as Tatum and out of action for a visit to his draft board. And to add to their frustration, they were missing those long-range baskets that were vital to their attack. Sanford played like he was trying to force his way into the Trotter lineup. Higlin and Doherty and that other O'Brien were gluing themselves to Trotters. Wheeler pushed through for a couple of layups,

Clarence Wilson got another and Robinson banged home a hook from the rim of the key, but the Chiefs led, 46–36, at halftime and nobody in the crowd went for popcorn for fear of losing his seat.

Louis "Satchmo" Armstrong, who was in town with his band, played a couple of choruses of "Baby, It's Cold Outside" as a contribution to the halftime entertainment and was so caught up in the excitement he stayed for the second half and missed one show downtown.

The Reverend A. A. Lemieux, S.J., president of Seattle University, must have experienced a surge of pride as his team moved out to the locker room. He may have recalled the days his athletes, now in the national spotlight, played in a dingy gym against small-college opponents.

Brightman and the O'Briens had changed that, and Father Lemieux may have been thinking of his first meeting with the twins. The innocents, who seldom had been farther away from South Amboy than Perth Amboy next door, had arrived at Seattle's airport at 2:30 A.M. with nobody to meet them. They took turns sleeping and guarding the suitcases, which contained hardly anything to interest a thief. A bus finally got them to the city and another dumped them at Twelfth and Madison. They were surprised that Seattle wasn't neck-deep in snow. Out of pure luck the first person they saw as they marched onto the campus was the Rev. A. A. Lemieux. He started to pass them by with a friendly nod, then gasped. "Oh no," he said. "You can't be the O'Briens."

Brightman had returned from a trip to the National Baseball Congress tourney in Wichita with an excited account of the New Jersey twins he found down there. Al begged that Seattle U., for the first time in its history, give out not just one but two full four-year scholarships.

"How big are they?" asked Father Lemieux.

61

"Oh, I dunno," said Al, casually, as if it didn't matter. "I guess about 6-3."

Fortunately, the tall, slender priest had a sense of humor and took an immediate liking to the Irish duplicates to whom his school had pledged four years of education. Juniors now, he had come to know them well. Johnny was the star, the one who got the headlines, the one who was to make most of the All-American teams as a senior, but the quieter Ed was also valuable to both his school and team. It was Eddie who threw in the final basket of the half from 30 feet out.

But the Trotters apparently were through fooling around with these kids when they returned for the second half. Tatum drove in for a layup on the tipoff, Bobby Wilson hit a long shot and then did it again after Johnny O had sneaked past Robinson for a layup. The Trotters were rolling. Josh Grider connected from long range, Tatum hooked one home from the right side, Wheeler swished a jumper from the side of the key and almost before you knew it was happening there went Milton on the fast break and the score was tied at 53.

Johnny was fouled by Milton and converted the point, but then Robinson took a pass under the basket and dipped the ball into the net. The Trotters were ahead for the first time in the game, 55–54, and there was hardly a person in the big old brick Pavilion who wasn't convinced that this was the end of the line for the audacious Chieftains. The curtain seemed to fall for sure 30 seconds later. Eddie had skipped through for a layup to put Seattle ahead again, but then Johnny O and Grider crashed and Johnny came up off the floor limping painfully. He hobbled to the free-throw line and sank the point, but he had to leave the game. And for the only time that night all the noise went out of the Pavilion as if sucked through a straw. There was a bit more than 2½ minutes left in the third quarter as Seattle called time.

Brightman huddled with his troops at the Chieftain bench after sending Les Whittles to report as a substitute for Johnny. "When I called you in for a special practice Friday and told you we were going to play the Trotters Monday," Al said, speaking softly, "I also told you we could beat 'em. The plan is still the same. Sanford will take the post while John is getting his ankle taped. Just run your stuff and remember"— he tossed them a grin as they bunched hands before breaking the huddle—"you're all I've got."

Robinson banked home a jumper from the side and the score was tied again at 57. Eddie tried a shot that bounced off the rim, but Doherty, jumping higher than he knew he could, tipped it in. "They've got us beaten on the boards," Al had said, "so we'll all go to the basket."

Robinson hit a free throw but Whittles took to the air to duplicate the Doherty tip-in. And then Doherty hit a jumper from the side and Moscatel sank a free throw. Eddie fouled Clarence Wilson, who got the point for the Trotters, but Sanford matched it just before the buzzer closed out the third quarter.

Seattle, 65; Globetrotters, 59.

"Why are you coming back?" Eddie greeted John as the bigger O returned with his ankle swathed in tape. "We were losing when you went out and now we're 6 ahead."

Brightman grinned, knowing Ed was the leader of the pair, the playmaker. For an instant he was back in Wichita, playing first base for the Mount Vernon, Washington, Milkmaids against the South Amboy Briggs. He had been convinced by a mutual friend that the O'Brien twins, who were being eyed by Columbia and St. John's, were worth going after. Johnny reached first on a single and Brightman, pulling a small notebook from his pocket, asked the puckish little guy if he'd care to attend Seattle University. The notebook said the twins had graduated from St. Mary's High School in South Amboy and were working in the summer in a pottery factory when not busy with baseball. "You'll have to take it up with my brother —he'll be along in a minute," said Johnny O, taking off on a steal of second base. And he was right. Ed walked and Al took up the conversation just where John had dropped it.

Seeing the little Irish artist back at his position as the final quarter opened, the crowd took another breath and regained its hysteria. Johnny O sank a jumper from the key and pulled the ball-between-the-knees trick on Wheeler. He watched Robinson sink a long one-hander for the Trotters, then led the fast break back down the court for an easy layup and the score was 71–61.

Wheeler fouled him on the play and left the field of battle with his sixth infraction. (During the third-quarter break the Trotters, with several players in danger of fouling out, had insisted on switching to the pro rule permitting six fouls. Seattle, also with starters in trouble, agreed.)

William Brown came in to guard Johnny, who picked up a couple more baskets, but things began to turn frantic on the court when the Trotters rallied and, with 5:10 to play, sliced the gap to 77–69 on a long shot by Robinson. Higlin fouled out of the Seattle lineup and Tatum hooked a right-hander for 2 more points. Sanford scored on the fast break but then fouled Tatum and the Goose collected the point. Robinson hit a long one-hander, then Milton scored on a set shot from beyond the key and the margin was 3 points, 79–76.

Johnny O got his first point in nearly 4 minutes after a foul by Brown, but the latter immediately made up for his mistake with a layup for the Trotters. Now they were down by only 2. Playing deliberately now, and with caution, the Chieftains maneuvered until they sprang Eddie for a layup. Tatum, fouled by Moscatel, made his twenty-third point and

Brown hit again on a tip-in. Now only 1 skinny point separated the teams, 82–81, with half a minute left.

Moscatel was fouled intentionally by Robinson to force the Chiefs to shoot and give the Trotters a chance to regain possession. Ray hit the first and missed the second, and in the scramble for the ball a whistle blew. An official had called a held ball and the Trotters asked for a time out.

"You've already used up all your times-out," said Hagerty. "I can give you another but it will cost you a technical foul."

For a reason never fathomed, the Trotters insisted upon the time out and Johnny O stepped to the line to shoot the technical. The crowd seemed to let all its breath go in a massive sigh as the ball arched and then the noise was rocking the place again as the twine snapped with the point that left the count at 84–81 with just 9 seconds on the clock.

The Chiefs put the ball in play and Doherty had it when the gun sounded and the crowd came surging on the floor like the cattle stampede in a TV western. Doherty howled in delight and pitched the ball so high in the air it wasn't seen for seventeen years—until the day a stranger brought the ball to Johnny as a belated gift. Scrawled in fading ink around the leather sphere were the autographs of all the Trotters.

At least 80,000 people have claimed they were there on the night the little guy scored 43 points and Seattle beat the Trotters, but here was a man with proof.

7

FORT WAYNE
FREEZE

Bob Fowler

•

•

The temperature was 16 degrees above zero and the blowing
snow made it seem even colder. This was Thanksgiving eve,
November 22, 1950, and most people in Minneapolis had
their minds on things other than basketball. Still, 7,021 of
them ventured to the Minneapolis Auditorium to see the
home-town Lakers, defending NBA champions, take on the
Fort Wayne Pistons. It was Father and Son Night—kids got
in for 50¢ if their fathers bought a full-price ticket—and
that in part accounted for much of the large turnout. A victory in this game would mean first place in the early-season
jockeying in the league's Western Division. The Lakers, who

*Minneapolis' George Mikan (99) was the only man
on his team to score a field goal. No. 19 is Vern
Mikkelsen.* WIDE WORLD PHOTOS

had won two NBA championships since jumping to the league from the National Basketball League, had a 29-game home-court winning streak extending over two seasons.

The Fort Wayne coach was Murray Mendenhall, fifty-three years old, with graying hair and described by one sportswriter as "a man as cocky as a bantam rooster who puts on a show all by himself with his bench antics." Before the game Mendenhall said, "There is only one George Mikan. I've been trying for three years to do something about him, but nothing works."

However, Mikan wasn't the only problem posed by the Lakers. True, he was the team's center and the center of those outstanding championship teams. And he was the man acclaimed as the greatest player in the first half of the century. He was leading the NBA in scoring with a 27.4-point average and used his 6-10, 240-pound size to dominate play, rebounding and intimidating anyone who got near the basket.

The Lakers also had 6-5 forward Jim Pollard, perhaps the club's best all-around player; 6-7 Vern Mikkelsen, another bruiser who got practically every rebound Mikan didn't; "quarterback" Slater Martin, one of the league's top-scoring and playmaking guards; and Bobby Harrison, a scrappy and good-shooting running mate for Martin. In reserve were players like Joe Hutton, Arnie Ferrin, Herman Schaefer and Bud Grant. It was an outstanding team that was almost unbeatable on the court.

In plotting the pregame strategy, Mendenhall described the Laker style of play: "The Lakers play a zone defense, with Mikan, Pollard and Mikkelsen never moving from under the basket. It's illegal, but no one has ever called them on it."

He decided to try to get the big Lakers to move. This could be done, he figured, by having the Piston guards, Johnny Oldham and Jack Hargis, work one-on-one against the Lakers'

Slater Martin and Bobby Harrison, who were smaller. Then if Mikan, Pollard and Mikkelsen were forced to come out on defense, it would open the area under the basket for Freddie Schaus, Larry Foust and Jack Kerris.

The Pistons started the game by playing a slow, deliberate style of ball with a lot of passing far away from the basket. They wanted to draw Martin and Harrison out so Oldham and Hargis could start driving around them. The only problem was that Minneapolis was content to let Fort Wayne pass the ball around and waste good shooting opportunities. The Lakers refused to be drawn out on defense and chase the taller Piston guards. With 2 minutes remaining in the first quarter, Fort Wayne managed to get a 1-point lead and resumed its slow game—which looked to the disapproving Minneapolis fans like a stall—which it was. At the end of the period the Pistons led by the embarrassing score of 8–7.

When Fort Wayne continued its strategy in the second period and Minneapolis still refused to cooperate with the Piston game plan, the 7,021 fans were howling loud enough to cause referees Stan Stutz and Jocko Collins to go into a huddle. They knew of no rule that covered the situation, since the stall was legal, even though it was seldom used until the latter stages of a game. So Stutz and Collins weren't able to do anything to speed up the game. They pleaded with Mendenhall to have his team shoot, but the crafty coach countered with the argument that Minneapolis should be called for using the illegal zone defense.

The referees had no choice but to allow the game to continue. The Lakers rallied with 6 points in the quarter—the final 2 coming on a Mikan basket with 32 seconds remaining —to walk off the court at the half with a 13–11 lead.

Schaus described the Pistons' walk off the court at half time: "The fans were really irate. They were throwing everything

71

possible at Murray, especially those sitting in the balcony. The players had to surround him and escort him to the locker room so the fans sitting on the floor couldn't get at him."

In the locker room, Mendenhall was starting to have some second thoughts. He discussed the situation with the players. There was unanimous opinion—keep the slow-down tactics. After all, in past seasons when they tried to match the Lakers shot-for-shot and point-for-point in Minneapolis, the Pistons often trailed by several points at halftime.

Meanwhile, in the Lakers' locker room, coach John Kundla told his players to maintain their positions. "We've got the lead," he explained. "We don't have to chase them. There is no reason for us to foul just to get the ball."

In the third quarter, Fort Wayne outscored Minneapolis, 5–4, to cut the Lakers' lead to a single point, 17–16, entering the final 12 minutes of play.

There were only 2 points scored during the first 8 minutes of the final quarter: Pollard had sunk a free throw for Minneapolis and Fort Wayne rookie center Larry Foust, playing his first game against the legendary Mikan, had countered with a free throw. And so, with 4 minutes to play, the score was Lakers, 18, Pistons, 17, and Fort Wayne had the ball. The Pistons called time out. Mendenhall and his players then decided they would hold the ball for a final shot, and hopefully a good one to win the game.

In the other huddle, Kundla instructed his players to "give them the last shot, but make sure it's a long one." He added, "Don't foul them and give away two free-throw attempts, either."

The Pistons returned to the court and resumed their stall. A missed pass sailed out of bounds. Everyone in the arena screamed with delight, for it seemed obvious that Minneapolis would get possession. But Stutz and Collins ruled the pass had been deflected out of bounds by a Laker, so Fort Wayne retained possession.

The hooting and hollering that had been going on throughout the game rose to an almost deafening level. The fans who had anything left to throw—popcorn boxes, programs, pencils, paper cups—unloaded in the direction of the referees. Play had to be held up while the court was cleared of debris.

When "action" finally resumed, the Pistons held the ball until there were 10 seconds showing on the clock. Then guard Curly Johnson started for the basket. Foust cut across the foul line and Johnson hit him with a pass. Foust turned and started dribbling and manuevering toward the basket.

Mikan recalled what was racing through his mind as he watched Foust wheel toward the basket: "I knew he wanted to be fouled. I was determined not to touch him, and I didn't. He hooked a short shot—almost a lay-in, really—and I partially deflected it with my fingers. But it still went in."

Mikkelsen was standing behind Mikan, waiting for the rebound. "I saw George hit the ball, but there was no rebound."

There were 6 seconds showing on the clock with Fort Wayne now ahead, 19–18. Time was running out as the Lakers tried to salvage victory, winning streak and first place. Slater Martin received a pass at midcourt and fired from there. The ball hit the rim, but there was no time for a rebound as the horn sounded, ending the game.

The Pistons had succeeded in stopping Mikan and the mighty Lakers in Minneapolis. Records? The combined score matched the lowest single-team score in NBA history. Fort Wayne tried 13 field goals, making 4. Minneapolis was 4 for 18, all 4 by Mikan, who scored 15 of his team's 18 points. The Pistons hit on 11 of 15 free throw attempts, the Lakers

10 of 17. Fort Wayne grabbed 8 rebounds, the Lakers 9. Minneapolis' other 3 points were scored on 2 free throws by Harrison and 1 by Pollard. Johnny Oldham led Fort Wayne with 5 points. Paul Armstrong had 4, Fred Schaus and Larry Foust 3 each and Jack Hargis and Jack Kerris 2 each.

The game's aftermath was filled with controversy.

Charles Johnson, executive sports editor of the Minneapolis *Star and Tribune,* called the game a "sports tragedy . . . one of the worst exhibitions this game has ever known."

But Dick Cullum, a columnist for the Minneapolis *Tribune,* criticized the Lakers for not solving the Pistons' stalling tactics. He praised the strategy and wrote that the game "may have been the best basketball game ever played by the pros in Minneapolis."

Indiana fans were thrilled. Schaus recalled, "We took the train back to Fort Wayne that night and got in about 8 A.M. About a thousand fans were there to greet us. They had heard the game on the radio and were really happy."

Minneapolis fans were not as joyous. In the Minneapolis papers of November 23, some of the comments by fans included:

"I'll never watch Fort Wayne play again."

"So this is pro basketball? I'll never see another game."

"It was the best passing clinic I've ever seen. I'm sorry I missed the one on shooting."

Mendenhall defended his strategy. "We wanted to get those giants out in the open where we would have a chance to play, not get our heads knocked in," he said. "What was wrong with that? We won, didn't we?"

Kundla threatened to use similar tactics the following night during a rematch in Fort Wayne so that Indiana fans could see the kind of boring exhibition that would result. But both teams played it straight and the Pistons won again, 73–63. It was Fort Wayne's first two-game winning streak against the Lakers and its last as Minneapolis went on to take a third-straight division championship.

Kundla charged, "Play like that will kill professional basketball. There are other ways of beating us besides that. You could tell the fans didn't like it and they are the ones who pay the freight in pro basketball."

One who agreed with Kundla was Maurice Podoloff, then commissioner of the NBA. On Thanksgiving Day he demanded an investigation into the game's "irregularities." He also demanded to see Kundla and Mendenhall in his office along with referees Stutz and Collins.

"I don't want anything like that to happen again," he told team owners and coaches. "It seems to me that the two teams showed complete disregard for the fans in the type of game they played. In our game, with the number of stars we have, we of necessity run up big scores and when you get a 19–18 score, it's prima facie evidence that the regular type of game was not played."

The league's directors adopted a gentleman's agreement that such a game would never be played again.

8

THE CALVERLEY SHOT

Murray Chass

•

•

"C'mon, Ernie, get a move on or we'll miss the train."

Rushing was nothing new to Ernie Calverley, especially in the morning. He frequently would wake up late, giving himself barely enough time to get dressed, grab a quick breakfast and scurry to his first class.

But on this particular morning in Kingston, Rhode Island, March 14, 1946, he was rushing not to get to class but to get to New York. That's where the train was going, and that's where the National Invitation Tournament was. Ernie was going to the tournament with the rest of his Rhode Island

79

Ernie Calverley (3) was but a 145-pound wisp of a center for Rhode Island State against big Bowling Green. UPI

State teammates, and they were scheduled to play in the opening game that night.

As always when they had a game in New York, the Rams were taking the 8:25 A.M. New York-New Haven, and as usual, Ernie was rushing to make it. He did make it, of course, because neither the team nor the train was about to go anywhere without Ernie Calverley, the 5-foot-11 center around whom coach Frank Keaney's racehorse offense was built.

The Rams had been to the NIT the year before and advanced to the semifinals, where they ran into DePaul and George Mikan and emerged from the collision on the very short end of a 97–53 score. The 97 points were a Madison Square Garden record, as were the 53 points Mikan scored. Coincidentally, after Mikan and mates trounced Rhode Island, they whipped Bowling Green, 71–54, for the title, and it was Bowling Green that was to be Rhode Island's first-round opponent this time around.

In the intervening year the Rams had won 18 of 20 games, losing only to St. John's and the United States Coast Guard, while Bowling Green had amassed a 27–4 record. The NIT selection committee felt that both teams were worthy of return trips, but the Falcons were one of the first teams invited while the Rams were the last. But as the train sped toward New York, the Rhode Island players weren't thinking about the lateness of their invitation. They were thinking of the long day ahead of them and the task they faced toward the end of the day—the bigger, stronger Falcons. Further back in the train, in cars that had been added for the occasion, hundreds of Rhode Island students and fans thought about the game, too, but they also looked forward to the good time they would have in the big city.

Three hours and 15 minutes after the train left Kingston it chugged into Grand Central Station in New York. The players, twelve in all, took their bags and walked off the train, through the crowded station and out to Forty-second Street. There they piled into cabs and headed for the Paramount Hotel on Forty-sixth Street between Seventh and Eighth avenues, in the heart of Manhattan's show-business district. By taking a short walk they could have spent the afternoon at the Majestic Theatre watching the Rodgers and Hammerstein musical "Carousel," or at the St. James enjoying another Rodgers and Hammerstein hit, "Oklahoma." Or if they preferred a movie, the Paramount Theatre was showing Bing Crosby, Bob Hope and Dorothy Lamour in "Road to Utopia" plus a stage show featuring Benny Goodman and his orchestra. Among the other movies in the immediate area were "The Spiral Staircase," "The Lost Weekend," "Spellbound," "Sentimental Journey" and "The Sailor Takes a Wife," the last accompanied by Sammy Kaye and his orchestra plus Marie (The Body) McDonald. The players could have spent the afternoon at any one of those shows. But they didn't. Instead they spent the afternoon in their rooms because that was coach Keaney's policy. He was no Captain Bligh, but he was a realist. He wanted the players to concentrate on the game and nothing else. After all, that's why they were there. He wouldn't even let them sit or stand around the hotel lobby, as it was jammed with fans seeking tickets and information. He also had the telephones in their rooms cut off from incoming calls. So instead of acting like tourists, the Ram players formed into groups of three and four and lounged around their rooms. They talked, they played cards. They talked, they read. They talked, they slept.

They also listened to the radio off and on and heard that Joseph Stalin had called Winston Churchill a Hitler-like warmonger, that two major strikes—against General Motors and General Electric—had ended, that the stock market was down again and that Pete Reiser would play center field again for the Brooklyn Dodgers. Occasionally, a player would shuffle off to another room to see if the time was going any faster there.

A few thousand words and several dozen card games later, the players put their ties and jackets back on, regrouped and left the hotel for their pregame meal. It was a few minutes before 4 P.M. when Keaney led the group into Gilhooley's, a restaurant on Eighth Avenue just a couple of blocks from Madison Square Garden.

For Calverley it was a typical pregame meal—steak, potatoes, peas and a dish of ice cream. It would not be a typical game, though, because as the center of the team—and one of the smallest in the nation—he would face one of the biggest centers in the nation—6-foot-11½ Don Otten. Calverley was familiar with Otten, having played with him in the previous year's All-Star game in Chicago. But this was the first time the little man from Pawtucket would have to play against him in a game.

Bowling Green's offense, of course, was built around Otten, and the big man had responded with a 14-point-per-game average. The Falcons, as a whole, had averaged 63 points a game to the opposition's 41. Rhode Island, on the other hand, was going through a revolutionary process, having become one of the first teams to adopt the run-and-shoot style. Despite mounting criticism from basketball conservatives, the Rams raced up and down the court, threw floor-length passes and shot from anywhere at anytime. The result this particular year had been a 78-point average (they had surpassed the 100-point mark in three games) compared with 59 for the opposition.

Now, as the Rams—after another time-wasting stretch at the hotel—walked up Eighth Avenue toward the Garden, they thought about what they would have to do to combat the height advantage Otten gave the Falcons. Obviously they would have to get the ball, bring it down the floor fast and score frequently. Their major problem, though, was whether they could keep Bowling Green from scoring as often.

In the locker room, Keaney reminded his players of what they would have to do. "We can't play catch with them," the jovial 250-pound coach told his 12-point underdogs. "We can't bring the ball up slowly. We have to outrun them and keep that guy Otten from catching up with us."

The major share of the responsibility in keeping the attack going belonged to Calverley, the twenty-one-year-old son of a Rhode Island lace weaver. The task, of course, was not unfamiliar to Ernie, who was completing his fourth season of varsity basketball despite a heart murmur that had caused him to be discharged from the Army Air Corps after a four-and-a-half-month stay in 1943. There was, for example, the game in which he had his ankle stepped on. The ankle blew up like a balloon and the team doctor ordered Ernie to sit out the remainder of the game. In the second half, however, the Rams lost four players on personal fouls, leaving only four healthy players for the rest of the contest. Keaney didn't exactly know what to do until Ernie begged to be put back in, swearing he would stand only on his good foot. Keaney relented and his star did just that. He stood on one foot near center court and kept flipping in one-handers, finishing the game with 32 of the Rams' 48 points.

Ernie, however, had two good feet for Bowling Green, and he needed them because the Falcons, seeded second in the tournament, had their offense working as usual. Otten planted himself inside, just off the foul lane, and repeatedly took passes from his smaller teammates and jumped over his smaller opponents for baskets. And when the Rams converged on

83

Otten, trying to keep him from getting the ball, Tom Inman, a 6-foot sophomore, and Leo Kubiak, a 5-11 soph, would hit from the outside or the corners. But the other end of the court was just as busy. Hitting from the outside, Calverley and two others, 6-foot Al Nichols and 6-3 Bob Shea, kept the Rams in the game.

First the Falcons went out in front by a few points, then the Rams came back, tied the game and took the lead themselves. Then it was Bowling Green's turn again as the game see-sawed through the first half. The Rams couldn't keep Otten away from his basket, but he was too slow to keep up with them as they whipped downcourt to their basket.

The crowd, which was slowly filling the Garden for the doubleheader, at first was nonpartisan. Although the Rams were the underdogs, they also were the team that had been selected instead of CCNY, a local favorite. CCNY had come on strong at the end of the season, but Rhode Island already had received the last invitation. Thus many of the fans started the game with a hostile attitude toward the Rams. But when they saw the hustling, fighting, determined spirit of the New Englanders, they were soon converted to their side and applauded enthusiastically when Rhode Island left the court at halftime leading by a point, 35–34.

Fans continued streaming into the Garden, and by the start of the second half a Garden record 18,458 were in their seats and standing, ready for another torrid 20 minutes. And they got it. The Falcons continued feeding Otten, and the Rams continued to run, run, run, and the score remained close.

Calverley was even more brilliant than in the first half. Despite the Falcons' overwhelming physical strength, Calverley's poise, his speed, his slick passing, his uncanny shooting eye and his fiery spirit kept the Rams in the game. Each time

84

the Rams fell behind by 5 or 6 points, Calverley brought them back and even sent them out in front by scoring himself or passing deftly to Nichols and Shea for clear shots.

The lead kept bouncing back and forth, and the game was tied seven times. Otten continued to be the difference for Bowling Green as he dominated the boards. But he was incurring fouls, and with 3 minutes left—after he had scored 31 points—the giant Falcon was whistled out of the game with his fifth personal. The crowd roared its approval of the call by referee Lou Eisenstein, but the Rams weren't about to suddenly coast into the lead. They tied the game, 68–68, after Otten left, but the Falcons scored 6 of the next 10 points to lead, 74–72, with seconds to go.

After that last basket, Rhode Island quickly called time. Not permitted to go to the bench (under rules at that time), the players huddled near the center of the floor, some crouching, others kneeling on one knee, all breathing hard. They didn't say much, deciding only that Shea would throw the ball in bounds and Calverley would take the last shot. When the buzzer ended the time-out, Shea walked toward referee Eisenstein to take the ball at the end of the court. The other referee, Matty Begovich, walked to the other end of the floor and signaled Eisenstein to start the last 3 seconds of the game.

Shea fired the ball to Calverley just past the foul line. There wasn't even time for a dribble. The 145-pound center with the heart defect wheeled and heaved the ball with both hands, just as if he were taking a two-hand set shot from 25 feet— except that he was standing 58 feet away and he threw the ball a lot harder.

As the ball sailed toward the other end of the court it sent the frenzied crowd into silence, the Rhode Island players into hopeful prayer and the Bowling Green players into hopeful

His teammates and spectators carried Ernie Calverley off the floor in a triumphal procession. UPI

confidence. From some angles of the Garden the ball didn't look high enough. From other angles it didn't look as if it would go far enough.

But the ball was high enough, and it sailed far enough. A second later it dropped directly through the basket, never touching the backboard, never touching the rim.

When they realized what had happened the fans and the Rams went wild. The buzzer joined in the pandemonium, sounding the end of regulation time with the game tied, 74–74.

Calverley didn't score a point in overtime, but he didn't have to. The underdog Rams outscored Bowling Green, 8–5, and the last team invited to the NIT was the first to win, 82–79.

When the final buzzer blared, the Rhode Island players leaped into the air. Keaney rushed for Calverley, wrapped him in his chunky arms and kissed him on the cheek. Simultaneously, a mob of hysterical fans swarmed onto the floor and engulfed their hero. Those closest to him lifted Calverley to their shoulders and carried him triumphantly off the court.

It would be a great train ride back to Kingston the following morning—if the Rams made it. They were willing to wait for Ernie Calverley no matter how late he slept. After all, his 58-footer was the longest field goal ever made at the Garden.

9

MAN OF THE CENTURY

Sandy Padwe

•

•

The date was December 8, 1961, and Wilt Chamberlain had scored 78 points in a game against the Los Angeles Lakers. Chamberlain was with the old Philadelphia Warriors and his coach was a New York Irishman named Frank McGuire. McGuire was angry after the game. The Lakers had three, sometimes four men guarding Chamberlain, and McGuire had a running argument with the officials that night about keeping the Laker players "off Wilt's back."

"He'll get 100 points someday," McGuire said, his voice quivering with anger. After McGuire had grown a bit calmer

91

This is the basket that made Wilt Chamberlain the "Man of the Century" one night in Hershey, Pennsylvania. WIDE WORLD PHOTOS

he wondered about what he'd said. Was it really possible for a basketball player to score 100 points in a game?

Of course, 7-1 Wilt Chamberlain was used to hearing his name associated with 100 points. People had been predicting he would score that much in a game since his days at Overbrook High School in Philadelphia and at the University of Kansas. So as the 1961–62 NBA season progressed, McGuire's statement was forgotten as the Warriors vainly tried to catch the Boston Celtics, who were leading the Eastern Division.

On March 2, 1962, the Warriors were scheduled to meet the last-place New York Knickerbockers in Hershey, Pennsylvania, 102 miles northwest of Philadelphia. The Warriors trained in Hershey before the season and played a few league games there every year, usually as part of a doubleheader with the Harlem Globetrotters appearing in the first game. As always when the team traveled to Hershey, the players would meet at a central location and take a chartered bus to the Hershey Arena. On this cold, dreary winter day, they were scheduled to meet at the Sheraton Hotel in downtown Philadelphia at 3:30 P.M. Soon the bus was on the Schuylkill Expressway, heading north toward Valley Forge and the Pennsylvania Turnpike. By 5:30 P.M. it pulled into a parking lot behind the Hershey Arena and the players, clutching their duffel bags, their coat collars turned up against the winter air, straggled into the building.

On this day the Globetrotters were not part of a doubleheader. Instead there was a preliminary game matching players from two professional football teams—the Philadelphia Eagles and the Baltimore Colts. In the Eagle lineup were such names as Timmy Brown, Irv Cross, Tommy McDonald, Clarence Peaks and Pete Retzlaff. The Colts countered with Gino Marchetti, Bobby Boyd, Bill Pellington, Jim Mutscheller and Carl Taseff. A few of the Warriors watched the preliminary game for a few minutes and then tired of it and strayed to the rear of the Hershey Arena, where there was an amusement area featuring pinball machines, strength tests and the like. Chamberlain began playing one of the machines and soon lights were flashing and bells ringing. Wilt, who had often been called a scoring machine himself, was now beating the mechanical monster.

Gametime was 8 P.M. and the players began drifting into the locker room, where trainer Bill Bates taped ankles and attended to the minor aches and pains accumulated during the long season.

By seven-forty the teams were on the floor going through their warmup drills and most of the crowd of 4,124 fans had settled into their seats. Some read the Warriors' official program, titled the "Wigwam" and edited by sports announcer Dave Zinkoff. Staring at them from the front cover was Wilt Chamberlain.

There was nothing unusual or unique about either team's pregame warmup. As the music came over the loudspeaker, the players went through their methodical preparations, first two lines for layups, then the usual semicircle with players taking outside shots as they tested the floor and lighting.

A few minutes before the start, the officials—Pete D'Ambrosio and Willie Smith—came on the floor and then went to the scorer's table, where they made last-minute preparations and checked to make sure that the rules met NBA standards on this neutral court. Then the game started. And so did Wilt Chamberlain. At the end of the first period he had 23 points and Darrall Imhoff, the Knick center subbing for the injured Phil Jordan, already was in foul trouble.

Chamberlain added 18 points in the second period for 41 at halftime. Eddie Gottlieb, the Warrior owner, sensed that

93

Wilt was headed for one of his greatest scoring nights "because he was making his foul shots, too." Imhoff was having great difficulty with Chamberlain as was Cleveland Buckner, a slender forward who had also been assigned to guard him. Chamberlain was awesome, powering his way underneath for layups, scoring on his famed fall-away jump shot and tipping in missed shots.

The fans began to sense that something important was about to happen when Chamberlain added 28 points in the third period for a total of 69. Wilt already owned the NBA's single-game scoring records with 78 points in the three-overtime game against the Lakers on December 8, 1961, and with 73 in a regulation-time game against Chicago on January 13, 1962. Both marks seemed certain to be broken this night. Wilt quickly broke one of them with three quick baskets at the start of the fourth period to give him 75 and the chant "Give it to Wilt! Give it to Wilt!" filled the court. Shortly after the fourth period began, Imhoff fouled out, so 6-9 Buckner and 6-7 Willie Naulls tried to contain Chamberlain. Other Knicks sagged on him trying to help Buckner and Naulls, but it was wasted effort.

With 7:51 left, Guy Rodgers fed Chamberlain and Wilt hit a fall-away jumper at the foul line to give him 79 points, a record. Now the Warriors realized that Wilt had a good chance to score 100 points, so they decided to feed him even more. The Knicks, however, desperately tried to avoid it by holding the ball for the full 24 seconds whenever they took possession.

With 5 minutes remaining, Chamberlain had scored 89 points. Now the Knicks tried a new strategy—fouling other members of the Warriors before they could pass the ball to Chamberlain. McGuire retaliated by sending three substitutes into the game, Joe Ruklick, Ted Luckenbill and York Larese, whose job it was to foul the Knicks, enabling the Warriors to get the ball in return.

Chamberlain did not score again until only 2:45 remained. Then he made a foul shot, added two more free throws and then connected on a long fade-away jumper for 94. Another fade-away, on a pass from Rodgers, made it 96, and then with 1:19 remaining, Larese fed Wilt a high pass and he dunked the ball through the basket. Now the fans were on their feet and screaming. The players on the Warrior bench squirmed with the tension while the Knicks were in a state of shock.

Chamberlain intercepted the throw-in pass and missed a shot from the foul line. The Knicks then took possession, holding the ball as long as possible before their shot, which missed. Now Philadelphia came down court, Wilt moving into the pivot, surrounded by Buckner and Naulls and the rest of the Knicks. Ruklick fed Chamberlain, but Wilt missed. He grabbed the rebound and missed again. Then Luckenbill moved underneath, grabbed the ball and passed out to Ruklick, who spotted Wilt under the basket and lobbed the ball toward the hoop. Chamberlain jumped, grabbed the ball with both hands and stuffed: 100 points.

Forty-six seconds remained on the clock, but some 200 fans swarmed onto the floor to congratulate Chamberlain. After authorities had cleared the floor, Chamberlain's teammates, and even the despondent Knicks, shook his hand. In the dressing room, Chamberlain's teammates continued the celebration. "Tonight," McGuire said, "was a wonderful thrill. I remember the first time a team I coached scored 100. Now this. It's almost unbelievable. He deserves all the praise in the world."

A smiling Chamberlain then told reporters, "It took a lot of effort for me. But it was just as big an effort for the team. It wouldn't have been close to possible to do this if they didn't want it for me as much as I did. That's what makes it so important to me. They wanted me to do it, and so did the fans."

Paul Arizin, who at the time was the second-highest career scorer in the NBA, could not believe Wilt's performance. He stood shaking his head in the Warriors' dressing room. "I never thought I would see it happen when I broke into the league," he said. "It's a fantastic thing. I'm very happy for him."

Guy Rodgers wound up the evening with 20 assists. "There wasn't an easier way in the world to get assists tonight. All I had to do was give the ball to the Dipper," he said.

Al Attles, the backcourtman, had a perfect night from the field, 8-for-8, and quipped later to Chamberlain, "Big fella, I'll have a mental block the rest of my life. I don't miss a shot and nobody even talks to me."

Chamberlain then added, "It was funny. I never thought of getting a lot of points, but when I made my first nine fouls [he actually made ten in a row], I thought it would be great if I could break the record for most fouls in a game. But then going into the last quarter, we all knew I had a chance at the 73 and 78."

Chamberlain had an unbelievable—for him—night at the foul line, connecting on 28 of 32. He also set a number of individual records:

Most points, one game—100
Most field goals, one game—36
Most free throws, one game—28
Most shots, one game—63
Most field goals, one half—22
Most points, one half—59
Most shots, one half—37

96

Most points, one quarter—31
Most shots, one quarter—21

And so the team boarded the bus for the return trip to Philadelphia. Dave Zinkoff, who always made sure there was a supply of frankfurters, hamburgers, sandwiches, cold drinks and coffee loaded on the bus, had some extra helpings this night. It was the least he could do. After all, this was a rather special night.

10

ALL-STARS' ALL-STAR

David Schulz

•

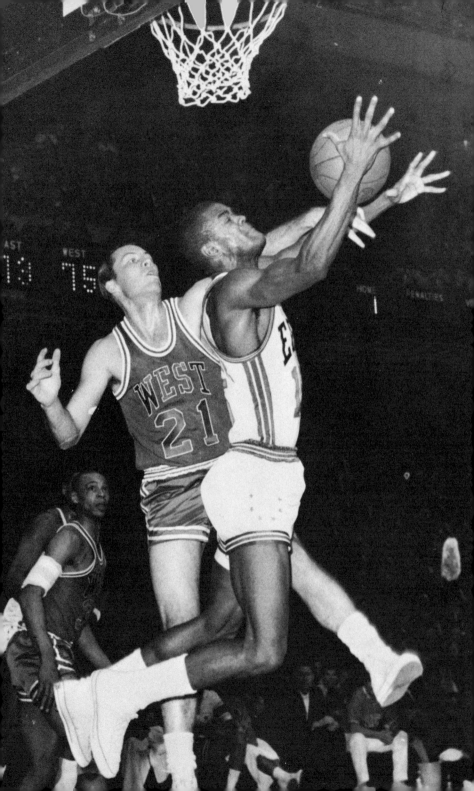

•

Hal Greer rested fitfully on the hotel bed. The cold, rainy New York weather affected the arthritis in his shoulder. He tried to think about something else, like the NBA All-Star game. After all, that's why he was in New York.

It was January 23, 1968, and for the third time in eighteen years the All-Star game was being played at Madison Square Garden. This was going to be the last one, however, played in the Garden located on Eighth Avenue between Forty-ninth and Fiftieth streets. A new, bigger Garden was being built about twenty blocks downtown in Manhattan.

But Greer, a thirty-one-year-old veteran guard with the

101

The East's Hal Greer goes up and the West's Jim King fouls the 76er in the All-Star Game.

Philadelphia 76ers, couldn't help but let his mind wander back to regular-season play. The 76ers were the defending champions, having ended Boston's long string of championships. And at the All-Star break—with less than 25 games to play— the 76ers were leading Boston in the standings by a game.

This would be Greer's eighth All-Star appearance. Of the players in this eighteenth game, only Boston's Bill Russell, Los Angeles' Elgin Baylor and Hal's 76er teammate Wilt Chamberlain had played in more. But, while they were called "superstars," Greer, if he was referred to at all, was usually called something like, "reliable Hal, the unsung hero." And reliable Hal knew he wouldn't be in the starting lineup.

Ever since he broke into the league with the Syracuse Nationals in 1958, Greer had been living out of the limelight. He was the Nats' No. 2 draft choice out of Marshall College, which few people had ever heard of. He managed an 11.1 scoring average as a rookie, but the Syracuse players who got the attention were ironmen Dolph Schayes and Johnny Kerr, and two-hand set-shot artist Larry Costello. The 6-2 Greer was just another cog in a machine that made the play-offs every year, but not until 1967 had it won a championship. Greer's aggressive play, quick jump shot and better-than-average field-goal accuracy won him a starting berth with the Nats. When his scoring average improved to nearly 20 points a game during the 1960–61 season, he was picked for the All-Star game for the first time. After that he became an annual choice, since his play remained consistent and he was lucky enough to avoid serious injury.

When the Syracuse franchise switched to Philadelphia, Greer moved along. The first season in the City of Brotherly Love, 1963–64, saw Hal's scoring average improve to 23 points a game. But those were the days when the Celtics were winning everything and the only backcourtmen you heard anything about were Sam Jones, the Celtic star, Oscar Robertson of Cincinnati and Jerry West of Los Angeles. Everyone knew how good Greer was—he was even called "the spirit of the 76ers"—but he was just taken for granted.

Then came Chamberlain. Big Wilt was traded from the San Francisco Warriors to the 76ers, and of course any time Philadelphia won, Wilt was the man who got the credit. It was Wilt and "four other guys" who beat the opposing team. It was with the help of those four other guys, though, that Wilt was finally able to be on a championship team, something that had never happened to him before in college or in the pros. And now one of those four other guys was getting ready to play in the All-Star game.

All the big names were there: Russell . . . Chamberlain . . . Robertson . . . Baylor . . . West . . . Lucas . . . Havlicek . . . Reed. They were all ready to do battle to determine—at least until next year—which division's players were better—or, at least which division's stars were better. For some players this was a once-in-a-career opportunity, or the signal that they were emerging into the star category. Making their first appearances in the All-Star game were Dick Barnett of New York, Dave Bing of Detroit, Bob Boozer of Chicago, Archie Clark of Los Angeles, Walt Hazzard of Seattle, Jim King of San Francisco and Don Kojis of San Diego.

But the record crowd of 18,422 had come to see the "regulars" like Bill Russell, who was making his eleventh appearance in the game. Chamberlain and Baylor were in it for the ninth time. Jerry West, like Greer, was an All-Star for the eighth time.

One All-Star was missing—San Francisco's 6-11 center, Nate Thurmond, who had helped the West upset the East last year. Thurmond was recovering from knee surgery. Warrior coach Bill Sharman, who was handling the West team, was forced to choose a forward to replace Thurmond. Sharman came up with 6-10 Clyde Lee, a second-year man from his own San Francisco squad. Lee moved to center for the Warriors when Thurmond was hurt, and he was being asked to do the same in the All-Star game.

Sharman also had to come up with a strategy to counter the East's two dominating centers, Russell and Chamberlain. He figured aggressive play—meaning a pressing defense and a fast-break offense—would be the only way.

East coach Alex Hannum, who masterminded the 76ers' 1967 championship drive, planned to start Chamberlain and use him throughout the first quarter, then play Russell in the second period. "We'll see who runs things better," Hannum said before the game.

Teaming with Chamberlain in the East starting lineup were Cincinnati's Jerry Lucas and New York's Willis Reed at forwards, and Oscar Robertson and Dave Bing at guards. Greer, as he had figured, started on the bench. The West lineup had the two Laker superstars, Baylor and West, combining with the three St. Louis Hawk representatives, center Zelmo Beaty, forward Bill Bridges and guard Lenny Wilkens.

Reed opened up with a 2-pointer for the East and the white-clad home team went on a 12–2 spree to establish a comfortable lead. Most of the New York fans were delighted and settled back to watch what they had been told would be an easy East victory. Robertson hit on 6 of 7 shots from the floor, and Bing chipped in a few points to give the East a 37–25 lead at the end of the period.

The starting lineups had stayed intact through most of the first quarter, but at the start of the second 12-minute session, substitutions were freely made. Boston's John Havlicek and Russell came in for the East. Sharman decided to use Lee against Russell at center. And Lee responded better than had been expected. Russell, the Celtic player-coach, was outscored 6 points to 2 and outrebounded 8 to 2 by Lee, while the West began to chip away at what had become a 14-point deficit. At one point, the red-shirted Westerners went on a 12-point binge while allowing the East a lone free throw to reduce the gap to 2 points, 52–50. Then Havlicek started hitting—he scored 12 points in the first half—to help the East to a 64–59 halftime lead.

After intermission, the coaches once again juggled their lineups. Beaty was back in at center and Jim King came off the West bench to team with Jerry West in the backcourt. Sam Jones and Greer—who had played for about 5 minutes in the first half and scored 2 points—were in at guard, and Chamberlain was back in the pivot position. Robertson and Bing had tailed off after their hot first quarter and Hannum hoped that the 76er teammates, Greer and Chamberlain, might get something started.

Hannum and his two stars decided to use the "C" play, the one they used so successfully at Philadelphia. Greer explained it: "It's simple enough. The guard passes into the corner, where the forward gives it back to the guard. The center comes out and sets up the pick and I go around him either way." By "either way," Greer meant that after getting the ball from Chamberlain—stationed away from the basket to block or "pick" Greer's defender—he could either drive for a layup or stop and take a jump shot from the free-throw circle. Greer had worked on that quick jumper, a shot that has almost no arc at all, since he was a kid growing up in Huntington, West Virginia. Huntington is a sleepy river and railroad town on the Ohio River where West Virginia, Ohio and Kentucky all come together. It is very Southern in many

105

of its attitudes and Greer went to an all-Negro high school. He was such a good basketball player, though, that Marshall College, located in Huntington, decided to integrate.

"I was the first Negro athlete to go to Marshall. It was strange, but being home helped. I had been on my way to North Carolina, to attend Elizabeth City State Teachers College, where my brother had gone to school. But I didn't have any trouble. It was just a challenge," Greer said.

And now he was facing another challenge. It was to get some points for the East All-Stars. But before he could do much, the West rallied, with Jerry West hitting three baskets in a row to give the West its first lead at 71–69. The teams traded baskets and with nearly 5 minutes gone in the third quarter, the West led, 75–73.

Greer, with the half-grin, half-scowl that covers his face when he plays, brought the ball upcourt quickly. Jim King was guarding him closely as he signaled to Wilt to try the "C" play. In a couple of seconds Greer hit on his jumper after a pass from Wilt, and the score was tied.

The next time the East had the ball, Greer didn't have to signal Wilt. They tried the play again. Again it worked, and defender King was shaking his head at the quickness with which the East regained the lead. The West missed another scoring opportunity and Greer once again brought the ball up, passed into the corner and worked the "C" play with Wilt. The dumbfounded King was caught flatfooted. Not only was Greer hitting his shots, but Wilt was showing why he was considered the best-feeding center in the league.

The 76er duo worked the play again. And again. In less than 3½ minutes, Wilt picked up 6 assists, Greer hit on seven shots in a row and the East had scored 14 points while the West converted only four free-throw attempts. Greer's shooting boosted the East to an 87–79 lead.

Lenny Wilkens came in for the frustrated King and Greer started passing the ball off. One time he hit Sam Jones with a pass that the Celtic star nearly dropped. Jones passed it right back. "I'd rather see him shoot," Sam explained after the game. Greer scored 5 more points—for a record total of 19 points in one quarter—and the East outscored the West 22 points to 6 to make the score 95–81. The West picked up a little at the end of the period to make it 101–91 going into the last quarter.

Hannum rested Greer at the beginning of the fourth period, and before Hal could get up again, Havlicek and Barnett were hitting from the outside to put the game out of reach. Greer stayed on the bench for the rest of the game as Hannum let everyone play in the 144–124 romp. It was the most points an East team had ever scored in the eighteen-game series and gave the East the lead in the series, 12 games to 6.

Greer got up again when the public-address system announced that he had just been voted the Most Valuable Player. The All-Stars' All-Star. He was finally getting some recognition. The fans stood and cheered as Greer received the trophy that had been given to such as George Mikan, Bob Cousy, Bob Pettit, Baylor, Russell and Robertson.

One of those most responsible for Greer's getting the honor was Chamberlain, who said he had been conscious of Greer's lack of recognition. "He has been a great guard," Wilt said after the game, "but he hasn't had the fame that he deserves. I must admit, I was looking to set him up if I could."

And King, who had to guard Greer, said, "He's tough, but when Wilt forces the split, he's even tougher. I was on Hal for 7 minutes. Wilt was looking for him. A couple of times I'd be between Wilt and Hal and he'd part my hair with the ball to get it to him."

John Havlicek, the game's high-scorer with 26 points, said,

107

Philadelphia's Greer and wife, Mamie, have eyes only for MVP trophy.   GEORGE KALINSKY

"I knew I was in the running for the MVP, but Hal deserved it. He went in when the game was close and the West had taken the lead. He broke it open."

Greer didn't talk much after the game. He did say of the large trophy: "I guess it's about the most enjoyable one I ever got." Then about his play: "I didn't do anything spectacular, nothing different from what I usually do."

And he was right. It is usually Hal Greer who breaks open the game for his team, getting the hot hand when it's needed. And it is Hal Greer who gets 20–25 points every game. He didn't do anything different in the All-Star game. It's just that this time . . . somebody noticed.

11

THE LONGEST GAME

Larry Felser

•

•

Normally Siena would be an anticlimactic stop on Niagara's annual downstate basketball visit and this time seemed to be no different. It might be even more anticlimactic than usual.

Madison Square Garden was the central reason for the trip, as the Purple Eagles usually had a generous dash of Manhattan and Brooklyn talent on their roster. Taps Gallagher, the Niagara coach, was Brooklyn-bred and a product of St. John's Prep and University. The Garden appearance was a bit of a homecoming for him each year. Only this particular year, 1953, it was a sour occasion. The Eagles seemed to be an ideal pick for the National Invitation Tournament, which then had a relatively exclusive field of eight teams. Niagara

Larry Costello got a new jersey with a new number.

NIAGARA

was a popular attraction in New York. Its record going into the game with St. John's was a good one. A showcase performance against the Redmen in the Garden would almost insure an NIT bid. But the performance was something less than showcase. St. John's did not have an especially strong team, but it managed to spoil Niagara's plans, 60–56.

So it was with something less than bubbling enthusiasm that the Niagara players took the floor of the Washington Avenue Armory in Albany for the Siena game two nights later, February 21. For them it was just an unwelcome layover on the glum train trip back to Niagara Falls.

The hundreds of students who had accompanied them to New York for the St. John's game didn't even bother to come up to Albany to root, preferring to remain in Manhattan for an extra night of fun.

For Siena, the game meant quite a bit more. A power in the lesser bracket of Eastern collegiate basketball, the disciplined, deliberate Indians reflected the personality of their coach, Dan Cunha. Cunha was a direct, honest person, scrupulously dedicated to the basketball matter at hand. When scouting another team, he did not write ahead for complimentary tickets in the press row, customary with most college coaches. Instead he paid for his own ticket at the box office, slipping quietly into a seat in the stands. Before a game he would ignore the opposing coach and his entourage until after the final whistle. Fifteen years later Gallagher would describe him as "the most underrated coach in America" at a testimonial dinner in his honor.

He liked to win.

Beating Niagara, considered a major power in the East, would be most satisfying to a competitor like Cunha and the 5,000 fans who packed the Armory. The Armory is a dank, airless place, more suited to sheltering tanks than housing basketball games. And there was a suspicion by visiting teams that the baskets and backboards, erected by Armory personnel just before gametime, varied wildly from the official height.

Just before the opening tap, Gallagher's assistant coach, Harry Condara, walked by a little-used reserve player, Frank Layden, as he was finishing his warmup shots. Layden was a native of Brooklyn, but Gallagher wasn't able to get him into the St. John's game in front of his friends and relatives due to its importance and closeness.

"We're gonna get you in tonight," Condara assured him. Layden, who would become Niagara's head coach fifteen years later, nodded his head, but silently resigned himself to his usual job of keeping statistics for the coaches.

From the start of the game Niagara is as cold as the chill atmosphere in the Armory. Siena, with its disciplined offense and two strong rebounders, Bill Hogan and Tom Pottenburgh, forges ahead. The Indians are a team that, when it takes a lead, can usually hold it.

Niagara, however, closes strongly at the end and the score is tied, 54–54, with time running out. Bo Erias, a tall, accurate-shooting forward, has fouled out of the game, but his replacement, Gerry Kennedy, is capable of getting a hot hand.

At last Niagara gains possession. Gallagher signals from the bench, putting his index finger high in the air. The Eagles know they are to play for the last shot.

Siena's defense also sees the signal. The Indians know they have to go after the ball, but without fouling anyone in the attempt. With 12 seconds to play they force a jump ball.

Niagara controls the tap. The ball goes to Jim McConnell. He jumps and arches a one-hander at the basket. It bounds off the rim, but Kennedy, following up McConnell's shot, drops in the rebound for a basket at the gun. A tremendously exciting finish and a 56–54 victory for Niagara.

But hold it!

Cunha is at the scorer's table. So is Gallagher. And the two officials, Clarence Jones and Frank Tabacchi. So are most of the players for both teams.

The 5,000 spectators don't know what's going on, but they aren't leaving their seats, either. Ten minutes of arguing pass before an official decision is reached.

The timer says—and is upheld in his decision by the officials—that Kennedy did not get off the shot before time ran out. The basket does not count. The score is tied, 54–54.

The game is in overtime.

Instead of holding the ball and playing for the sure basket in the overtime period, both teams employ an unusually aggressive brand of ball. With less than a minute remaining in the period, Siena holds a 59–58 lead as the Indians' Bill Kirsch steps to the free-throw line. His first shot hits the rim and drops through. His second shot goes through cleanly. Siena appears to be a sure winner.

But suddenly Niagara's young guard, Larry Costello, has the ball. Costello—who is to go on to become a professional star and eventually coach of the Milwaukee Bucks in the NBA—had a horrible first half, scoring but 1 point as his set shot was cold. But now he fakes a drive with his right foot, draws himself back as if to set, then breaks on a drive. The defender covering him bites for the fake set shot and doesn't recover in time to follow the drive properly. Desperately he fouls Larry, but not before the shot is launched.

The ball drops in and Jones signals that the basket is good. And Costello has a free throw coming.

The crowd holds its breath. Costello bounces the ball twice, then quickly flicks it toward the basket. The score is tied, 61–61.

Now both Gallagher and Cunha change tactics. Each tells his players to proceed cautiously, to play for the "sure" basket. Niagara gets its basket late in the period. Siena comes back, working the ball cleverly toward the bucket. Suddenly Hogan, who is built on the lines of a football tackle, thrusts himself along the baseline and up for the tying layup. The second overtime period ends, 63–63.

Enough is enough. The teams throw themselves into the next period briskly, with Jack Merry of Siena and Charlie Hoxie of Niagara the dominant players. But when the extra five minutes are finished, the score is again tied, 70–70.

It is getting late and everyone wants to go home—with a victory.

"Don't get loose," Cunha tells his players. "Stay with the deliberate style. Play for the good shot."

Over on the Niagara bench Gallagher is giving similar instructions. His emphasis is on the "good" shot. The Eagles missed badly in the previous period, taking some "bad" shots.

Neither coach has to repeat his advice. The players want this one over with, in their favor, as quickly as possible. The game has been going on since 9:15 P.M. It is now past eleven-thirty. Cunha and Gallagher are addressing weary performers. The players slouch, exhausted, on their benches, feet sprawled straight out to relieve the gnawing ache of overwork.

The next period, the fourth overtime, is to be a cautious one. Very cautious. Siena gets its basket with a point-blank shot. Niagara, almost immediately, retaliates for a 72–72 tie, which is how the period ends.

Now the rest period can't last long enough. Over on Siena's side the Indian trainer is tending to Hogan. Bill had a bad heel before the game and the four extra periods have him in near-agony. The trainer quickly retapes and repacks the heel and Hogan tells Cunha he's ready to saddle up again.

Gallagher stands in front of the Niagara bench and surveys his tired players. Costello and Ed Fleming have gone without relief for the entire game, but they look as if they can stick it out for another overtime session. Some of the others don't. Taps has to make a quick decision. He decides that he needs fresh players in the game.

"Layden," yells Gallagher.

The bespectacled youngster leaps off the bench and hands his clipboard to the coach for an inspection.

"Frank, I don't want to look at your statistics," says Taps. "I want you in this ballgame. Get your jacket off and report to the scorekeeper."

Before Layden can get in a word at the scorer's table, Frank Tabacchi poses an important question. "It's getting close to midnight," says the official. "Is there any local law says we can't continue after twelve o'clock?"

The coaches and school officials huddle quickly. It's determined that no such law exists.

"Let's play ball!" shouts Tabacchi.

This time the tactics change again. Each coach looks for the blitz, a final knockout. It's a question of endurance. Each wants his players to carry the action to the other team, to make one last effort to overpower the enemy.

Siena strikes first, with Tim Hill scoring on a drive. Layden, fresh and inspired, is fouled and drops in the free throw to cut Siena's margin to a single point, 74–73.

Niagara, at this point, is desperate for the ball. Too desperate. Hogan is fouled in the act of shooting. He steps to the line with his aching heel, but he is poised. Both shots drop in cleanly. It's Siena, 76–73, and the Armory is in pandemonium.

But the Indians are too anxious to hold that lead. Niagara's Kennedy dribbles to the outer perimeter of the key, where he is fouled. He sinks the shot and Niagara trails by just 2, 76–74.

The Eagles suddenly are in possession as the result of a Siena turnover. Time is called and Gallagher gathers his players around him for a strategy discussion, but Fleming— later to play with the Minnesota Lakers of the NBA—asks him to wait. There is a look of total discomfort on Fleming's face.

"Coach, I can't go on another second," says Fleming. "I've got to go to the john so bad I think I'm gonna die. My kidneys are about to explode."

"Eddie, the men's room is two floors down in this place!" says Gallagher, almost distraught. "Go over and ask the officials if they'll give you an extra minute or two in the timeout."

Fleming walks over to Tabacchi and Jones. They confer briefly, then shake their heads. "I'm afraid we can't," they tell him. "It's against the rules. Sorry."

Gallagher glances at the pained Fleming. Then he turns to his assistant, Condara. "Harry, go over to the Siena bench. Don't even ask. Just empty the Dixie cups out of that waste- basket and bring it here," orders Taps.

The assistant coach does what he's told. Gallagher takes the receptacle and tells his entire squad to huddle around him and Fleming on the edge of the floor. Ninety seconds later Fleming is ready to play basketball again.

Twenty seconds remain in the fifth overtime. The Eagles do not waste time working it in. Layden fires a jumper from less than 15 feet. It goes in. The game goes into its sixth overtime period.

It is now the longest game in college-basketball history.

119

Ed Fleming also got a new number.   NIAGARA

Layden's contributions seemed to have churned up the Eagle adrenaline. There's a freshness about Niagara that hasn't been apparent since the closing minutes of regulation play. They seem impatient to get the rest period over.

The tap goes to Fleming. He passes to Costello and Larry drops in a long set shot. Siena misses and Fleming rebounds. Costello comes up the side of the court, heads for the basket, stops and jumps. The Eagles are ahead by 4, 80–76.

Siena misses again, and it's fatal. The ball is passed to the still-fresh Layden. The tired Indian defenders can't keep up with him and he's in for a layup.

Niagara is in command, 82–76.

Hill drops in a jump shot for Siena, but Costello counters with another jump shot for an 84–78 lead.

Fleming drives for another Niagara basket. Hubie Brown drops in a free throw for the Eagles, and then Layden, who is to score a mere 12 points in his entire varsity career, explodes for a 3-point play, his eighth point in the last two overtime periods.

Fleming fouls out with less than a minute to play, but Costello finishes the game, a full 70 minutes of basketball. It's 12:17 A.M. when the final gun is sounded. The score is Niagara, 88; Siena, 81, in the longest college game ever played.

The next day Gallagher collects the jerseys normally worn by Fleming and Costello. He issues them new ones, 69 to Ed and 70 to Larry, in appreciation of their playing 69 and 70 minutes to make basketball history.

12

GUN FROM THE WEST

Bill Libby

•

•

In the fourth minute of the first game of the NBA's 1965 Western Division playoff finals, Elgin Baylor of Los Angeles twisted up for a shot and went down in a pile of pain. There was a loud pop that could be heard all over the court and which a Baltimore substitute admitted made him "sick." He said, "It sounded like the poor guy had broken his leg the way you snap a stick." Somehow, Baylor got up and began to chase the play toward the other end of the court, but he collapsed to the floor and the Lakers' championship hopes seemed to fold with him. Later he said that each step had

125

Los Angeles' Jerry West makes it in second game of the Western Division playoffs against Baltimore.

felt as though someone had plunged a knife into his left knee and was twisting it.

This was in the Sports Arena in Los Angeles in April at the conclusion of the 1964–65 professional basketball campaign. The more than 10,000 Laker fans in attendance suddenly hushed as they shared this moment of misery with their team and their fallen captain. Jerry West remembers looking at the stricken star and turning away, cursing in his disappointment and frustration. The Laker coach, Fred Schaus, remembers looking at Baylor suddenly all awkward with agony and wondering how long he might be out and thinking it would be hard, if not impossible, to win the game—much less the series—without him. Buddy Jeannette, the Baltimore coach, remembers watching Baylor helped off the court and thinking, "We have them now. We have them." While it is not sporting to take spirit from a foe's injury, it is an honest revelation of human nature. "I don't ever want to see anyone hurt, much less a great star like Baylor," Jeannette said, "but I'd be lying if I said it didn't boost our chances."

The Lakers had gone into the series heavily favored. They had just won their third Western Division title in four seasons, beating out St. Louis and Baltimore. The were considered the most formidable challengers to the domination of the league by the Boston Celtics, who were playing off in the Eastern Division. The Lakers had an outstanding team, but what made them outstanding was the presence of West and Baylor, who had averaged 31 and 27 points per game, respectively, during the regular season. The remainder of the club was ordinary. The centers and other forwards were Rudy LaRusso, Leroy Ellis, Gene Wiley, Darrall Imhoff and Don Nelson. There was no powerful big man. The other guards were Dick Barnett, Jim King and Walt Hazzard. Barnett was a great shooter. But the fact remained that Schaus loaded a two-barrelled shotgun.

126

The Laker style was to get the ball to forward Baylor or guard West and let them carry it. Without them, the Lakers could not even have made the playoffs.

Meanwhile, Baltimore seemed to be developing a powerhouse. The Maryland club had big, tough forwards in Bailey Howell and Gus Johnson, a strong center in Walt Bellamy, and skillful guards in Don Ohl and Kevin Loughery. The Bullets lacked quality depth on their bench, but they were bigger, stronger, younger and had better balance than the Lakers. The Bullets had begun to mature late in the campaign, had knocked a stunned St. Louis team out of the first round of the playoffs in an impressive upset, 3 games to 1, and now, with Baylor hurt, suddenly seemed certain to win this series, too. One could almost sense a surge of confidence passing among them during the time-out that followed Baylor's injury.

Meanwhile, Laker coach Schaus huddled with his men. "We'll all have to try harder," he said. Later, West recalled: "What else could he say? What could anyone say? You can try harder. And sometimes you can do far more than you think you can do. But our high hopes had been broken by Baylor's bad break." All athletes want to win, but there may never have been an athlete who wanted to win more than West. Unusually dedicated and intense, he was an outstanding player almost always, but at his best when it counted the most. Nicknamed "Mr. Clutch," which would later be the title of his autobiography, he probably has won more games in the closing moments than any other athlete in any sport. He was then—and remained later—the only pro basketball player ever to average higher during full playoff series each season than he did during the preceding regular season.

Uncommonly quick and graceful, West was not only the most gifted of ball-hawking defensive guards but a superb ballhandler and perhaps the finest shooter the game has known

127

—deadly with medium-range jump shots, splendid on driving shots, sure on free throws. Small by pro standards, and fragile, he was so often busted up by the giants of his profession that it seemed almost certain that sooner or later he would be carried off in pieces, yet he continued to play the game with almost reckless abandon, especially under pressure. And now he faced the greatest challenge of his colorful career.

West has said:

> Basketball games can be dominated by one or two men. It takes teamwork to win games and the best of players needs considerable help to win championships, but I'd be lying if I said I didn't realize that Baylor and I were the key men on the Lakers, the ones who had to share the greatest amount of the burden, the ones the others looked to for leadership, especially in times of trouble. I don't mind. The challenge inspires me. I want the ball when we need a basket. I know there are good players in this league who don't want it at tense times. They're afraid of failing. But I want it. I know I'll score.

After Baylor was hurt, he said, "I knew it was all on my shoulders now. I knew the guys would be turning to me. I got very determined. I began to play with all the fury I had in me. I worked and worked and worked and when I felt too tired to take even one more step, I pushed myself further."

The rest of that game, West seemed to be everywhere at once, stealing the ball, moving it, shooting it, scoring with it. Defensively, the Bullets collapsed on him and bruised him but they could not stop him. Inspired by him, Barnett and King and Ellis played as well as they had ever played. Stunned by this sudden, unexpected onslaught just when they thought things had turned their way, the Bullets fell 19 points behind.

After taking stock of the situation at halftime and realizing they should beat a Laker team without Baylor, they rebounded fiercely in the second half and pulled to within 2 points with time running out.

West brought the ball upcourt, fed a perfect pass to Ellis and Leroy rammed it in. Baltimore came back as Bellamy sank a free throw and Loughery knocked a Laker pass free. But West dived daringly into a scramble for the loose ball, came up with it and dribbled away most of the remaining seconds until he was fouled. He sank two free throws and it was all over. At the final buzzer, L.A. had won, 121–115. West had scored 49 points.

Having won the opener, the Lakers now awaited word on Baylor. It could not have been much worse. Part of his knee-cap had torn away. He was to undergo surgery immediately. He was out for the series. He would be lucky ever to play again. (He would, and brilliantly, but none knew that.) The news struck all of the Lakers hard. They could visualize themselves winning a big game or two without Baylor, but not a big series against a strong and hungry foe. Facing the fact of the loss of his accomplice in basketball artistry depressed West deeply, as though fate had deprived him of the laurels he wanted so desperately. He resolved to give it his best, but later confessed what he would not then tell his teammates—that he considered their cause hopeless.

Two nights after the opener, in the Baltimore dressing room, Jeannette told his Bullets, "Jerry West is a great player, but he is just one man. He can't beat us all by himself. We have great players on our team. We could have beaten them with Baylor. We certainly can beat them without him." But they did not. It was a tight, tense contest throughout. Already weakened by the loss of Baylor, the Lakers were weakened further when LaRusso fouled out. Wayne Hightower hit two

129

free throws and the Bullets led 115–114, with 38 seconds remaining.

The Lakers brought the ball back and West tried a jump shot from 8 feet, but it missed. As the ball came off the hoop the 6-11 Bellamy and the 6-10 Ellis leaped and wrestled for it. West somehow surged into the fray, leaped among the giants, wrenched the ball from their grasp and, as they came apart, lobbed it over the fingertips of the jumping Bellamy and into the basket to reclaim the lead for L.A., 116–115. It was one play in one game, a single move in the midst of madness, but many will never forget it. With 21 seconds to play, Baltimore set up a play. The ball was passed to Ohl. West lunged, knocked it free to Nelson. Nelson returned it to West. Jerry was fouled. He sank two free throws and the Lakers won, 118–115.

West had scored 52 points, the second-best total of his entire career and one topped only by Baylor and twice by Wilt Chamberlain in the history of NBA playoffs. After missing his first free throw, he had sunk twenty in a row. He had played 44 of the 48 minutes and with the help of 24 points by Barnett and 20 by LaRusso had negated the determined efforts of Ohl, Loughery, Bellamy and Johnson, each of whom had scored between 20 and 30 points each for Baltimore. Outside the depressed Baltimore dressing room, Jeannette promised the Bullets would pull even in the next two games when they got to their own home court.

As the series shifted into the ancient city of Baltimore on the shores of Chesapeake Bay, the advantage seemed to shift to the Bullets. Many felt the Lakers had won the first two games on desperate desire, but were bound to be used up now. Without Baylor, it was estimated that not even West could continue the sort of heroics that would deny the Bullets much longer.

And in the third game, the Bullets did go on the aggressive, bruising the Lakers badly. On one play, Bailey Howell kneed West in a nose that had been broken seven times previously, and Jerry played the remainder of the contest with cotton stuffed in his nostrils to stem the flow of blood. His record string of successful free throws was snapped at 31 and, though Jerry wound up with 44 points, Howell, fighting off muscle spasms in his back, led the Bullets to a 122–114 victory.

Now the tide seemed to have turned. In the fourth game the Lakers, already thin without Baylor, were further thinned by the loss of Barnett, sidelined with a pulled groin muscle. Bellamy, Johnson and Ohl banged away at the troubled visitors. In the late stages, Ohl sank shot after shot. Still, West sparked a stubborn resistance that refused to let the Bullets pull away. He didn't miss a free throw and scored 48 points— and it was almost 50. In the clutch, the Lakers trailing by 2 in the closing seconds, West moved, jumped, shot and hit. However, even as he had been moving, LaRusso had been moving, too, striving to screen Ohl and colliding with him. Referee Joe Gushue blew his whistle and called a foul on LaRusso, nullifying West's tying basket. The Lakers sagged in disappointment at a heartbreaking loss, 114–112. Now the Bullets were even, 2 games each.

On a Sunday night in Los Angeles before more than 15,000 fans, the two teams tangled in the fifth game. For a half it was tight. Barnett returned, but unable to move to either side, he had to plough straight ahead. Still, he teamed well with the rugged LaRusso to support West splendidly. West appeared tired in the first half as the Bullets several times seemed on the verge of breaking the game wide open. However, after the break he returned to score 17 points in the third period to break Baltimore's back. Jerry wound up with another big bag

131

The saddest man in the Los Angeles Sports Arena was injured Laker Elgin Baylor, sitting next to Rudy LaRusso.

of 43 points as Baltimore was beaten, 120–112, and the Lakers were within one game of victory.

As the two teams flew cross country, the Lakers were weary, the Bullets angry. It is difficult to win on the other team's court, but many felt if the Lakers did not win in Baltimore, the Bullets would win the finale in Los Angeles. The Bullets were healthy and in a mean mood, determined to atone for their disappointing showing thus far against a crippled team. The Lakers, meanwhile, were almost spent. All had played beyond themselves. All were tired. Barnett could hardly walk. West's nose was badly swollen. He had a slash across his cheek, a knot as big and purple as a plum on one thigh, his whole body was bruised.

No matter how long he plays or how well he does, West gets worked up emotionally for every game. He sulks through game days, no good to himself or his family, his muscles tightening, his nerves fraying, his temper shortening as the pressure mounts and thickens within him. Now, in his hotel room in Baltimore, he squirmed restlessly on his bed as the last hours moved slowly. Finally it was time to go to the arena. In the dressing room, West gulped pills, as he always does to abate the sickness that sweeps over him. Now he hung on the very edge of nausea. The strain of striving to sustain an incredible pace distressed him.

The stage was set. It was a Tuesday night, April 13, and the 8,950 fans crowded into Baltimore's Civic Auditorium set up bedlam from the opening tipoff. Television cameras beamed the critical action back to hundreds of thousands of Southern Californians. Baltimore cruised out in front immediately and after 10 minutes led by 13. At the quarter they led by 10 and were given a standing ovation as they went to their bench for the brief break. But West, who loosens up with the opening tipoff, was unwinding now. And King, sent in by the desperate Schaus, gave him an unexpected lift. In the second 12-minute session, the Lakers counterattacked successfully. They drew even at 42-all, then outscored the Bullets, 7–1, in the final 75 seconds of the half to take a 6-point lead to the dressing room.

The Lakers collapsed in weariness in their quarters, while across the way the Bullets were being roused by Jeannette. "Pull this one out and we'll win the series," he told his men. The Bullets virtually burst onto the court for the second half. They hammered at the Lakers, who braced for a while but then began to weaken as bedlam broke out in the big building. Isolated on the brightly lit hardwood floor, the players were soaked with sweat and bathed by noise as they battled it out. Bellamy and Howell bashed away up front. Ohl and sub Wally Jones sent off sparks. Somehow West summoned the stamina to lead a determined but diminishing resistance.

With less than 4 minutes to play and the Bullets trailing by 2 points, the Lakers shot and missed. Bellamy rebounded and immediately fired a long pass to the fleet Ohl. Unguarded, he crossed midcourt and drove toward an unprotected goal as the crowd cheered, counting the score. Ohl jumped to shoot—and at that instant, seemingly out of nowhere, West leaped, reached out a long arm and in one motion blocked Ohl's shot, took the ball and pulled it to his gut. A great groan sounded from the crowd. West twisted, dribbled away, hurried back downcourt and threw the ball high toward the basket. Tall Gene Wiley jumped, caught the ball and stuffed it. Now the Bullets trailed by 4 with seconds to play. They hurried the ball back and the Lakers let Howell have an easy one at the final buzzer and won the game, 117–115. They had won the series. And the fans filed out quietly.

In that final game, West scored 42 points, set up 16 more

with 8 assists, grabbed 8 rebounds and stole the ball five times. In none of the six games had he scored less than 40 points. His per-game average was 46.3, and he had totaled a record 278 points, a record which was bound to endure. In just eleven nights he had played to inspired perfection six times to give a performance unmatched by any player in any single series in the history of the sport. He had single-handedly inspired a good team to greatness under the most trying of circumstances and the most intense sort of pressure. And he had so demoralized the Baltimore team it would be years before the Bullets rebounded to the verge of glory.

In the noisy, joyous clamor of the Laker quarters, a worn and weary West admitted, "I wouldn't have done what I did had Elg been playing. I wouldn't have had to." Later he admitted, "I was exhausted. I felt absolutely drained and worn out. I had nothing left for Boston."

He had enough left to score 45 in one game and 43 in another game against Boston, but no one could beat those Celtics—not even the brilliant Jerry West. The Celtics won in five games. It's odd, though. What people remember about the 1965 NBA playoffs is not just another of many Boston triumphs, but the triumph of one man and his short-handed mates over a good team.

13

THE LAST CIGAR

Bob Sales

•

•

April 28, 1966, was Red Auerbach's final day as coach of the Boston Celtics. The final game of the final playoff series played against the Los Angeles Lakers that night at Boston Garden was the 1,585th he'd coached in twenty seasons on NBA benches. And the final victory was one Auerbach wanted so badly he could taste it.

The Celtics were going for their eighth-straight league championship and their ninth in ten seasons. They had finished second to Philadelphia in the East—the first time they hadn't

A familiar Celtic cast—Satch Sanders (far left), Bill Russell (6) and Sam Jones—lines up for Elgin Baylor in the final game. UPI

won the division title in nine years—and they came back to beat the 76ers in the playoffs.

Auerbach woke up early on his final day as a coach. He looked around his suite at the Hotel Lenox, in which he'd lived during the past sixteen years. There were several letter-openers, a key to the city, two television sets. There was some cold Chinese food in the refrigerator. He decided to skip breakfast.

Auerbach drove to the Celtics' offices at the Garden, parked his car in the street and went to work at his other job—that of Celtic general manager. The phones were busy all morning, which was good. It kept his mind occupied and his hands busy. He did not spend all day thinking about the game.

Around noon he decided to eat something. A salami sandwich wouldn't stay down. He went back to answering telephones. And waiting. Someone suggested that Auerbach take a nap in midafternoon, but the forty-eight-year-old coach balked at the idea.

"I don't see any purpose in it," he said. "I want to keep going. I don't want to relax. I want to be hungry. I want to be concerned, grouchy, brusque, but not nervous. Certainly not calm. I want to be up."

At five o'clock, three hours before gametime, Auerbach called his wife at home in Washington.

"How do you feel?" asked Dot Auerbach.

"I feel like it's the last game," he replied.

"It's been an awful long time. But it will be over soon."

"Yeah. Ten-thirty, eleven o'clock. But I can't remember a day when the hours dragged like this."

"Do you want me to come to Boston. I can still make it."

"No, baby. You don't want to see this one."

"I'll be watching. It's a beautiful way to finish. Wish the boys luck for me."

"Luck won't do it. They'll have to do it with their hands and feet."

The next three hours dragged by. Then it was time to get ready. It was time to head for the cramped dressing room, scene of so many Celtic victory celebrations. What could Auerbach tell his team? The newspapers had been full of "Win one for Red" headlines. This couldn't be his pitch—never had been. Auerbach felt that ballplayers ultimately had to win for themselves. Besides, these ballplayers were professionals. They would not rise to any sort of emotional pitch because of a pep talk.

Auerbach looked around the room.

Bill Russell, picked by Auerbach to be the next Celtic coach, veteran of every one of the championship teams, dressed in the corner. Russell was grouchy. That was good. He played best when he was grouchy. K. C. Jones and Sam Jones, the complementing twins of the backcourt, sat in front of their lockers. John Havlicek, young then but still a veteran pro, promoted to a starter in midplayoffs and now a star, sipping tea. Satch Sanders, the quiet defensive star, dressing slowly. Don Nelson, picked up for nothing in midseason and a valuable addition, smiling crookedly.

"This one means about $700 apiece to you guys," said Auerbach. "That's the difference between the winners' and the losers' shares. Can you show me any other way you can make $700 in 48 minutes? And remember this: If you don't win it, you'll have to spend the whole summer answering stupid questions. Ask Russ and K. C.—they were on the team when we lost the title to St. Louis in '58. They had a beautiful summer. So did I. I want you to win this one for you, not for me."

That was the end of the pep talk. A professional addressing a group of fellow pros. But it wasn't all that Auerbach had

141

to say. Gail Goodrich, a rookie backcourtman for the Lakers, had been a major annoyance to the Celtics throughout the series. He'd been driving successfully on the Celtics, unheard of ever since Bill Russell joined the team. He'd scored 28 points in the sixth game at Los Angeles as the Lakers tied the series at 3 games apiece. He had to be stopped.

"That kid's a cool rookie," said Auerbach. "I don't want him to be an important part of the ballgame. Let's concentrate on him the way we do on Elgin Baylor and Jerry West. Don't get careless with him or relax for a minute because he can take the title away from you."

Auerbach turned to Sam Jones. "You hear me good?"

"I hear," replied Sam.

"You stay in that kid's shirt," Auerbach said.

"Thanks," said Sam.

Then the players were on the court, taking their warmup drills, and the coach was in front of the bench, a folded-up program in his right fist. The minutes ticked by. Finally, the teams were introduced and the game started.

Russell flicked the opening tap to K. C. Jones, who flipped the ball to Havlicek cutting toward the basket. The Celtics led, 2–0. Then Sam Jones scored two straight baskets. Then Sanders. Then Sam again. The Celtics led 10–0. It was beautiful. The Lakers didn't score until more than 4 minutes had elapsed.

The Celtics led by 7 at the end of the first period. The clawing, hustling defense was superb. The fast break, ignited by Russell's rebound and outlet pass, was sizzling. It was lovely. The Celtics led, 53–38, at the half. Moments into the second half they led by 19—their biggest bulge of the game. And it was 76–60 going into the final period.

The capacity crowd was jovial. Only one dramatic moment

remained. Auerbach traditionally lighted a cigar when he decided that a game was won. At what moment would he light up? Auerbach had been in the game too long to be over-confident, and that was doubly true in the playoffs.

When an out-of-bounds call went to the Lakers, Auerbach slapped at the ball. The people in the stands chuckled. Good old Red. He'd always be the same.

With 4 minutes left the Celtics led by 13. But the Lakers weren't quitting. Two baskets by West and one by Rudy LaRusso cut the lead to seven.

The Celtics came downcourt and worked the ball to Sam Jones, guarded by West. Sam passed to Sanders. The Celtics were using up time. Sanders passed to Havlicek, who dribbled left and flipped the ball to K. C. The 24-second clock was ticking away. K. C. popped and missed and Leroy Ellis rebounded for L.A.

The Lakers came back downcourt quickly, working the ball to West, who missed. The ball rolled out of bounds. Now the Celtics worked the ball downcourt to Sam Jones who flipped a lead pass to Russell, who stuffed the ball to extend the Celtic lead to 91–82 as the game entered the final 2 minutes. The ball exchanged hands several times before West made 1 of 3 free throws with 1:16 to go. The Celtics now led, 91–83.

A 35-footer by Sam Jones was matched by a 15-foot jump shot by Walt Hazzard and the score was 93–85. There were 42 seconds left when Russell stuffed to make it a 10-point lead.

"The crowd is starting to go berserk," announcer Johnny Most reported to his radio audience.

The crowd was surrounding the court, hanging on the

143

fringes, wanting to be in on the kill. The celebration was starting too early.

"Thirty seconds left," said Most, losing his voice, "and the Celtics are on the verge of their ninth championship."

West hit a long jumper for the Lakers. So what:' There were only 16 seconds left. Auerbach stuck the cigar in his mouth and turned to John Volpe, Governor of Massachusetts, who offered a light. The crowd surged onto the court and leaned on the supports of the baskets. Auerbach pleaded with them to leave, to let the game end peacefully.

The pass went to K. C., who tried to work his way past Hazzard and was whistled down immediately. Offensive foul. Lakers' ball with 14 seconds left. The crowd was still on the floor. Sam Jones' smile froze on his face. Auerbach was jumping up and down behind the crowd, trying to see what was happening on the court.

"The crowd has surged down to the sidelines," Most reported, "and they can't finish the ballgame. They have asked the crowd to get back. They are trying to move them back now. They finally do."

Hazzard threw the ball in to Ellis, who passed to Jim King for a layup. The score was 95–91 with 9 seconds left.

The pass to Sam Jones was deflected out of bounds, but Sam had touched it last. Lakers' ball again, 6 seconds left.

The pass went to Ellis.

"A quick jump shot," said Most. "It's good! Four seconds left. The lead is down to 2 points. K. C. with the ball. Gets surrounded. One second. *That's it. All over.* Havlicek gets the ball and he gets mobbed."

Auerbach's lit victory cigar was lying on the court, crushed and forgotten. Five minutes later Russell and Auerbach and Havlicek and the game ball emerged from the throng intact.

In the safety of the dressing room, Auerbach lit another

cigar and started to savor the ninth championship, his 1,037th victory as a professional coach. It had been a typical Celtic victory.

Russell had 32 rebounds and 25 points. Sam Jones scored 22 and Havlicek 16 in a hustling, bustling, typical 48-minute performance. This was the offense. Defense was the difference.

West led the Lakers with 36 hard-earned points, dogged by K. C. Jones at every step. Elgin Baylor worked and worked and came up with 18, thanks to tenacious guarding by Sanders. Goodrich made only 6 points. LaRusso had 7.

"What a defensive game we played," said Auerbach. "We can't compare with them offensively when they have Baylor and West in there. You never can relax when they get hot. We played disciplined ball. We looked like a well-coached ball club." He said it proudly. "I feel drunk," he screamed, "and I haven't even had a drink."

Fred Schaus, the Lakers' coach, felt like he had a hangover, and he hadn't had a drink either. This was the fourth time he'd led the Lakers into the final round of the playoffs against the Celtics. Twice they'd taken them to seven games. The Lakers still hadn't won a title.

"Who ever thought 95 points could win the championship game?" Schaus muttered. "Ninety-five points. If somebody said to me you're going to hold them to 95 I would have known we were in."

He wouldn't have known that his team would manage to take only 88 floor shots—and make only 35 per cent of them.

"We couldn't hit," said Schaus. "It was a combination of our being off and their defense rushing us into bad shots. When my two big men don't hit . . . well . . ."

Auerbach posed with the game ball and Russell tossed him in the shower. Auerbach flicked cigar ashes on Russell. Then the room was empty—except for Auerbach. He picked

145

Red Auerbach has three most valuable possessions for his valedictory—cigar, ball and Bill Russell. UPI

up the ball and donned a dry practice jersey. He put on his coat and headed for the street, king of the basketball world. He was the toast of all Boston. Well, maybe not all. When he got to the street there was a ticket on his car.

14

CHAMPS OF THE ASTRODOME

Jeff Prugh

•

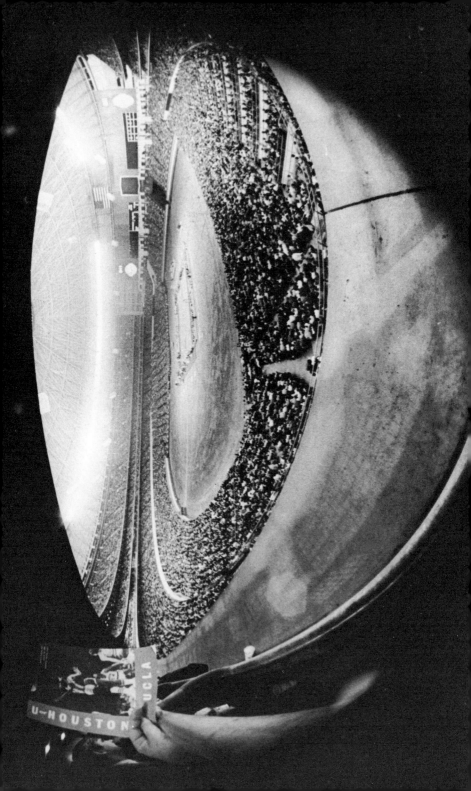

●

They were tall and gangly, college athletes all, and one stood
7 feet 1½ inches without even wearing his sneakers. But if
you watched them from those expensive seats that the man-
agement called "sky boxes"—which were nine tiers up—
they looked like ants crawling across a 6¢ stamp.

The setting was one of the most spectacular, if not unreal,
in the history of sport—a basketball game, of all things, in
the Houston Astrodome, of all places. There were bright
lights and thunderous cheers; there was this Texas-sized
scoreboard that flashed animated cartoons and spewed fire-
works; and there was this portable wooden floor, which looked

151

A record crowd of 52,693 jammed Houston's Astro-
dome for Big A vs. Big E.   UPI

terribly lonely out there on a field where football players roam in the fall and baseball teams play in the summer.

But this was a historic midwinter evening—January 20, 1968—the night of college basketball's Super Game. The confrontation could not have been better conceived by a Hollywood producer, and the drama could not have unfolded any better on the back lot of Warner Brothers Studios.

In one corner was Lew Alcindor, 7-1½, and the UCLA Bruins, who hadn't been conquered in almost two years and who were considered by many to be the mightiest college basketball team ever assembled. In the other was Elvin Hayes, 6-8, and the Houston Cougars, a team long on muscle and aspiration and a team that had not lost a game since it last played UCLA, which was nearly a year earlier.

For more than a year the Texans had been snapping up tickets faster than free passes to the State Fair, and by game-time the Astrodome would be jammed with 55,000-plus fans (52,693 paid), by far the largest crowd ever to watch a basketball game indoors.

"When I was in school, we used to play our games in a little place called 'the Barn,' " said John Wooden, the UCLA coach, reminiscing about his Indiana boyhood as he stood on the Astrodome floor. He looked high up into the glare of the floodlights above and said, "It's hard to imagine that a basketball game would ever be played in surroundings like these."

It was the night before the showdown, and the coach was sending his No. 1-ranked UCLA team—the defending national champion and winner of 47 games in a row—through a one-hour workout.

The players were already accustomed to the floor (it was the one on which they had played a few times in the Los Angeles Sports Arena and it had been shipped to Houston at

152

a cost of $10,000 because the Astrodome had no basketball floor). But it was debatable whether the Bruins (13–0) or the No. 2-ranked Cougars (16–0), winners of 26 out of their last 27 games, would be able to adjust to the cavernous surroundings.

"It should be an interesting game," said Wooden, "but it's very possible that both teams won't shoot very well—that's because the background is so different in here."

It was true. The Astrodome was not built for basketball— at least, it seemed that way to the players. It was somewhat like playing outdoors, since the seats seemed miles away from the court, thus giving them little backdrop when they shot at the basket. The interior of the dome is so vast, in fact, that the 28-story Los Angeles City Hall, if placed on the center of the floor, would not even touch the ceiling. And if the physical characteristics of the Astrodome were not exactly conducive to good basketball, they likewise weren't suited to basketball watching. The press had the best vantage point (from a trench that was dug around the floor at court-side), but the paying customers were so distant from the action that the nearest seats (the field boxes) were no closer than 100 feet from the court. As one Houston player said before the game, "We'll be worn out just running from the dressing rooms to the floor."

Watching the game from the stands, it was like viewing a silent movie. You could follow the ball, all right, but you couldn't hear the patter of feet or the bounce of the dribble. And the crowd noise, despite the sellout, was quieter than the sounds inside a packed gymnasium; the cheering sort of swirled around inside the giant dome.

Nonetheless, the game was as much a novelty as it was a milestone. Binoculars sold like hotcakes. Of course, the game figured to be a sellout, matching as it did Alcindor and Hayes, two of college basketball's most celebrated players ever. The game had been in the planning stages for almost two years and the mushrooming interest in it had grown to such a point that 150 television stations carried the action to cities as far away as Fairbanks, Alaska.

It was also the richest game of all time (a nonpaying crowd of 75,000 saw the Harlem Globetrotters perform in Brazil in 1951). Receipts grossed between $150,000 and $200,000, counting television revenue. The gross was divided equally between the two schools, except for roughly 17 per cent, which went to the sports association that leases the Astrodome from the county. Indeed it was going to be a grandiose production —something that only a bunch of Texas millionaires seemingly could have staged—but these were two very special basketball teams and the fans came by the thousands to see if UCLA was as unbeatable as so many observers had said it was.

The Bruins had not lost a game since February of 1966 and they had just brought John Wooden his third national championship in four years. They epitomized the Wooden style beautifully—run, attack and gamble on offense, press and harass the enemy to distraction on defense. That was the formula through an unbeaten thirty-game season the previous year and it was working to perfection through the thirteen games prior to the showdown at the Astrodome.

If a favorite had to be picked, it was obviously UCLA. After all, the Bruins had conquered Houston, 73–58, in the NCAA semifinals the previous year and now most of the players on both those teams were back. Lucius Allen and Mike Warren, a pair of astonishingly quick guards, made the UCLA fast break a devastating weapon, as they had in

1967. Allen, 6-2, moved with the grace and flow of a mini-Oscar Robertson and was to wind up the season as the team's second-leading scorer and rebounder behind Alcindor. Warren, a 5-11 senior, was a skillful playmaker—quick of hand and foot. The starting forwards were 6-5 Lynn Shackelford, a deadly left-handed shooter whose outside jump shots looked like the first stage of Apollo 11, and 6-6 Edgar Lacy, a senior who had sat out the previous season with a knee injury and who excelled with an assortment of squirmy inside moves and as a rebounder. And what's more, UCLA was equipped with a better corps of reserves than was Houston. On the Bruin bench were 6-7 Mike Lynn, a senior forward who was a starter on UCLA's 1966 team and who, like Lacy, had sat out the 1967 season; 6-7 Jim Nielson, a junior forward who specialized on defense and the backboards; 6-3 Kenny Heitz, a starter at forward the previous season; and 6-3 Bill Sweek, a swingman whose exciting, pell-mell style was deployed to pick up the tempo.

The star of stars, however, was Ferdinand Lewis Alcindor, Jr., whose presence did most to make the Bruins the extraordinary team they were. For a 7-footer, Alcindor was astoundingly quick and agile, perhaps more so than any center who had ever played the game. He wasn't only a star, he was a legend—a deep-thinking young man from New York City who spoke out against injustices toward his fellow black people and a player so good that collegiate rulesmakers had taken away the stuff shot from him (and everybody else) after the 1967 season. It was Alcindor's presence—intimidating on defense, overpowering on offense—that made whatever team he played for a prohibitive favorite. He had played on a losing side just once in five and a half basketball seasons (his high school team, Power Memorial Academy, had its 71-game

155

winning streak snapped in 1965, his senior year), and he was really the main reason why the UCLA–Houston extravaganza was booked in the beginning.

There was, however, a quite unexpected circumstance surrounding Big Lew's presence in this, his biggest of all appearances. Eight days before, in a game against California at Berkeley, an opposing player accidentally poked Alcindor in the left eye, scratching the surface so badly that he had to spend most of the week recuperating in the UCLA eye clinic.

In the days that immediately preceded the showdown at Houston, there was some doubt as to whether Alcindor would be able to play at all against the Cougars. Finally, two days before the game, he was released from the clinic and was permitted to practice briefly, with a thick bandage covering the eye. The following day, on the morning of the Bruins' departure for Houston, doctors removed the bandage and said it would be safe for Alcindor to play.

Meanwhile, amid all the speculation over Alcindor's availability, Houston coach Guy Lewis was proceeding right along in pregame preparations as if nothing at all had happened to Alcindor. "We're going to assume that he'll play," said Lewis, "because that's the only way you can prepare for UCLA."

Four starters who had played the previous year against UCLA would be back playing again in the rematch. There was 6-9 center Ken Spain, a strong-armed junior who was tough under the boards; 6-5 guard Don Chaney, who had arms like an octopus and excelled at stealing the ball from enemy guards; 6-7 junior forward Theodis Lee; and, of course, the Big E, Elvin Hayes.

After the first UCLA–Houston meeting, Hayes had made headlines by contending that Alcindor was "overrated." But

156

this time he was more complimentary. "It's on defense where he really hurts you," Elvin said. "He can make you give up the ball—and you can't make him commit himself."

Elvin Hayes, a twenty-two-year-old senior, came out of the cotton-country town of Rayville, Louisiana, where he grew up shooting baskets through a bucket that was nailed to a tree in his backyard. He was strong and aggressive around the basket, but he also had a velvet shooting touch from outside —and now he was ready for the biggest game of his life. And he spoke with customary self-assurance about the game ahead.

"They won't be able to get away with collapsing on me," said Hayes. "Nobody can. We've got too many other good shooters and, besides, I can always overpower one guy." UCLA, he said, was by no means invincible.

On the eve of the tipoff, John Wooden, having been told that Alcindor had "some double vision," was minimizing the effects of his star center's injury now that the doctors had given him permission to play. "I have very few reservations about him now," said the Bruin coach. "In fact, I'm most optimistic." Aside from Alcindor's presence, Wooden felt that his team had other things going for it. "Houston is as physical a team as has ever played in college," he said, "but I like to think we will have the edge in quickness and conditioning."

And was there pressure on his team? "Yes," he said, "especially when you figure that there will be less pressure on Houston. We have that long winning streak, you know."

Finally, the long-awaited showdown arrived. There were portraits of each player flashed on the scoreboard as he was introduced. The scoreboard was big enough to keep a running tabulation of fouls and points for each player (a basketball

It was the classic confrontation at the tip-off, UCLA's Lew Alcindor (left) jumping against Houston's Elvin Hayes.   UPI

"first"). And most of the 55,000 spectators, wildly cheering their beloved (or adopted) Cougars, hastily focused their binoculars.

After the opening jump, Hayes threw up a 25-foot jump shot —swish!—and the Cougars had scored the first basket of the game and the crowd went deliriously crazy. The two teams battled pretty much on even terms through the opening minutes, much like they had in their 1967 meeting at Louisville. It was 8–7, UCLA, before Alcindor hit his first field goal— on a drive from close range—and UCLA led, 10–7, when the game was not quite 5 minutes old.

It was obvious that Alcindor was sluggish and timid under the basket, apparently the result of his having been hospitalized. That seemed to take the sting out of UCLA's normally high-speed game—and George Reynolds, a competent 6-4 guard who had transferred to Houston from junior college during the off-season, had very little trouble beating UCLA's famed pressing defense.

From the outset, both teams seemed tense and edgy. Houston, also a running team—but not in UCLA's class—had managed to slow down the tempo, but there were numerous missed shots that should have been made and there were several turnovers on both sides. The only player performing at maximum efficiency was Hayes. Suddenly he beat his defender, Edgar Lacy, downcourt on a sneak fast break and poured in a layup. Then came a long jumper from the corner 22 seconds later and Houston had forged ahead, 11–10.

Mike Warren countered with a couple of free throws, giving UCLA the lead, 12–11, but Houston then reeled off 8 straight points with a torrid outside-shooting attack. First came two jumpers by Reynolds, then a bank shot and a jumper by Hayes, who kept eluding Lacy and getting open in the left corner. Now it was 19–12, Houston, and UCLA had not trailed by that large a margin in more than a year. The first half had not quite reached the midway point and the roaring partisan crowd was sensing that history might be in the making.

Indeed it appeared that way. UCLA, failing to move the ball quickly against Houston's 1-3-1 zone defense, was guilty of more turnovers and Alcindor was not playing with his customary finesse and zeal. Except for a goal-tending basket by Lucius Allen, the Bruins went 4½ minutes without a field goal as the Cougars slowly pulled away.

It was Lynn Shackelford, looping in a fall-away jumper, who finally broke UCLA's cold spell, but Houston was clearly in command, 21–16, midway through the first half. Then, with crackling suddenness, the magic of Elvin Hayes came thundering back. He unleashed another jumper—swish!— then stormed in for a layup, and swished in still another jump shot, all in the brief span of only 41 seconds, and Houston was coasting again, 27–16.

It took 8 points in succession by Shackelford and Allen to keep UCLA within striking distance, 27–24, but now the question was: How were the Bruins going to stop Elvin Hayes? The game was only 11½ minutes old and already the Big E had blistered UCLA's man-to-man defense with 16 points.

Wooden removed Lacy and replaced him with Mike Lynn. But UCLA went another 3½ minutes without a field goal, and there was still no stopping Elvin Hayes. With the score 31–26, Hayes began piercing UCLA's inner defense as neither Lynn nor Alcindor was able to fight him off. First he hauled down an offensive rebound and shoved in a field goal to make it 33–26, then came three more layups in rapid succession and a corner shot by Chaney as Houston stayed in front 41–36.

160

Only two long field goals by Lynn kept the Bruins in the game, but before the half was over Hayes made two more field goals—a tip-in and a jumper—and wound up with a whopping 29 points. At the half, Houston led, 46–43, the Bruins having made a last-minute run at the Cougars on an Alcindor hook shot (his second field goal of the game) and two baskets from long range by Shackelford and Allen. Though Houston's lead was tenuous, it was obvious that UCLA would have a difficult time preserving its perfect record. Houston was effectively shutting off UCLA's fast break, and unless the Bruins could find a way to guard Hayes, history would indeed be made.

As the second half began, Houston was nursing 3- and 5-point leads, and Mike Lynn soon found himself in foul trouble trying to stop Hayes. When Lynn committed his fourth foul, he was removed and Jim Nielsen became the third man assigned to Hayes—who had picked up his fourth foul with about 12 minutes left in the game.

Still, Hayes stayed in, and it was Chaney and Reynolds who took up the scoring slack. UCLA, however, managed to tie the game, 54-all, with 10:18 remaining on a long jump shot by Mike Warren. But then came still another UCLA cold spell—4 more minutes without a field goal—before Warren popped in another jumper.

Now there were but 6 minutes left. UCLA was jabbing and uppercutting—and Nielsen was doing a splendid job guarding Hayes—but the Bruins had yet to strike with the second-half fury that had been their hallmark for the past one and a half seasons. In fact, it was almost miraculous that UCLA had a chance to catch Houston this late in the contest. The Bruins were playing the kind of game Houston wanted them to play —deliberate and, at times, erratic. Lew Alcindor had added

161

only two field goals (matching his first-half total) and was scarcely a factor on defense.

It appeared that UCLA might finally make its move, however, when Lucius Allen stole the ball and streaked downcourt for a layup to cut Houston's lead to 63–61 with 4:46 to play. But a layup by Hayes made it 65–61 before UCLA quickly tied it, 65–65, on a short jumper by Nielsen and free throws by Warren and Alcindor.

Now the clock showed 3 minutes left and the plot was thickening. It was either team's game now, and what the game lacked in artistic refinements it certainly made up in drama. Within the next minute, Houston opened a 4-point lead, 69–65, on a Hayes bank shot and a Chaney jumper. UCLA, its attack having been smothered by Houston's zone, now began exploiting the quickness of Lucius Allen from close range, where he had played as a forward in high school. And the strategy worked. Allen, whirling and leaping amid a forest of taller Cougars, scored on a twisting layup and was fouled by Lee. He missed the free throw, but the Bruins trailed by only 2 points with 1:41 to play.

At the 1:05 mark, Alcindor committed his first foul of the game. It was an obvious ploy to send Houston's worst free-throw shooter, Ken Spain (56 per cent), to the foul line. And it worked, as Spain's free throw missed and UCLA got the rebound still trailing, 69–67.

The Bruins called time and again planned to spring Allen free under the basket. With 44 seconds left, Allen drove and was fouled in the act of shooting by Spain. That gave him two free shots and Allen, with the roar of more than 50,000 Texans cannonading through his ears, made both shots to tie the game for the fourth time, 69-all.

The game was now beginning to have that overtime look as

162

the Cougars slowly maneuvered the ball downcourt. They looked again to Elvin Hayes, the guy who had carried them this far, and with 28 seconds left he sliced across the foul lane under close guarding by Nielsen. As Hayes went airborne for a shot from close range, Nielsen, caught slightly out of position, reached out and slapped the ball in what appeared to be a clean block. But official Bobby Scott whistled a foul. Now it was again up to Elvin Hayes. He promptly dropped in points 38 and 39 of a night to remember and Houston was ahead again, 71–69.

Now it was UCLA's ball in an apparent time-out situation. But the Bruins, with only 25 seconds left, did not call time and quickly crossed midcourt. The seconds were ticking away and the place was bedlam as Lucius Allen, closely double-teamed by Chaney and Reynolds near midcourt, suddenly rifled a cross-court pass, apparently intended for Shackelford, an excellent shooter who was alone in the right corner. But the ball sailed wildly between Shackelford and Warren and went out of bounds. It was Houston's ball—with 12 seconds left— and the crowd began pouring out of their seats and onto the field.

Houston hastily called time out to talk strategy. When play resumed, the Cougars inbounded the ball to Hayes under the UCLA basket. Three blue-shirted Bruins swarmed around him, hoping to pry the ball loose or cause him to pass it wildly. But Hayes managed to get off a looping pass to George Reynolds near midcourt as the final horn sounded.

The game was over. Pandemonium. The stars were big and bright in Texas, and UCLA, the team that many people had predicted would not be beaten as long as Lew Alcindor was in uniform, was beaten at last. And Elvin Hayes was carried to the dressing room.

At the finish, there was a question of whether Houston had violated the 10-second rule, inasmuch as Hayes took so long to unload the ball to Reynolds. But it probably would not have mattered much, because UCLA would have been given the ball with only 2 seconds left—hardly enough time to make the tying basket.

The score was history, 71–69. Alcindor had played on a losing side for the first time since 1965, Allen for the first time since 1963, early in his junior year. The winning streak of 47 games—the second longest in collegiate history—was shattered just 13 victories shy of the University of San Francisco's mark of 60.

"We just got beaten by a better team," said Lew Alcindor, who had spent the dreariest night of his career (only 4 of 18 from the field, 15 points and 12 rebounds). "No, my eyes didn't bother me," he said in response to a question. "But I didn't feel physically good."

Said Guy Lewis, the Houston coach, in a dressing room that throbbed with soul music from Elvin Hayes' record player, which was turned up full blast: "I never thought we could beat these guys. This was my greatest victory."

Meanwhile, John Wooden was asked by a reporter to compare Elvin Hayes with Lew Alcindor. "I wouldn't trade Lew for two Hayeses," he said. "Hayes is a great player, but there are a lot of great 6-8 players." He talked about the night that was, a night when Big Lew was obviously off his game and UCLA shot only 33.6 per cent from the field. "This is a game," he said, "that will be good for our team. Not only that, but it was a great thing for college basketball."

In a couple of months, Houston and UCLA figured to meet again in Los Angeles—in the NCAA semifinals—and already people were speculating on what might happen if the game were to materialize.

164

"They call the Houston Astrodome the eighth wonder of the world," wrote Loel Schrader in the Long Beach (Calif.) *Independent-Press Telegram*. "But a victory by Houston over UCLA in Los Angeles would be the ninth."

The game did indeed materialize as expected. The score: UCLA, 101; Houston, 69.

15

SYRACUSE'S EASTER PARADE

Arnie Burdick

•

●

Even the Easter Parade was different that day. People poured out of church and in all their finery headed right for the Onondaga County War Memorial.

That's where the action was going to be that afternoon—April 10, 1955—as the local heroes, the Syracuse Nationals, were going to have their "showdown" meeting with the Fort Wayne Pistons for the professional basketball championship of the world. And there wasn't a red-blooded fan within shouting distance of the four-year-old, fancy downtown structure who wanted to "see" this one from the outside.

After all, these rabid Syracuse fans had suffered through

Syracuse's George King attempts the last free throw of the championship game against Ft. Wayne.
BOB JOHNSTON (SYRACUSE POST-STANDARD)

imminent escape from "sudden death" the day before in the best-of-seven series of the NBA's final round. The hot-shooting Pistons had led by as many as 10 points in the second half as they staged a determined bid to squeeze out a fourth-straight victory and gain the coveted crown. But the battling Nats were able to wiggle off that hook, 109–104, to knot up the series at 3 victories apiece. It took a courageous stand for coach Al Cervi's men to pull that one off, for they also had to survive a second-period riot that saw the hall turned into mass bedlam. During that scuffle, both benches emptied and spectators poured on the court after Syracuse's Paul Seymour and Wally Osterkorn and Fort Wayne's Bob Houbregs exchanged blows. Adding to the boisterousness of the occasion was a halftime melee that took vigorous police efforts to quell.

Referee Sid Borgia, knocked sprawling during the earlier skirmish, got swatted by another psyched-up customer as he tried to get to his dressing room during intermission. But he and his partner, Mendy Rudolph—thanks to the cops—finally achieved the privacy of their inner sanctum.

It was this kind of a charged-up atmosphere that greeted these two superbly conditioned, though drawn, teams as they readied for the opening center tap. Coach Charley Eckman's classy Pistons, led by rugged (6-9, 250) Larry Foust, smooth George Yardley and the fiery Frankie Brian, had eliminated the perennial champions, the Minneapolis Lakers, in the semifinal round of the playoffs. Meanwhile, coach Cervi's resourceful Nats, sparked by the tireless Dolph Schayes, the combative Seymour, the flashy ballhandler George King and the pivot-shooting rookie Johnny Kerr, were ousting the Boston Celtics in four games. (Schayes and Foust were selected to the All-NBA first five that season, with Seymour picked for the second unit.)

Thus it was an implausible matching of the league's two

170

smallest cities—Syracuse and Fort Wayne—playing for basketball's biggest prize.

The stage was set, and now after nearly six months of wearying travel and competition—after a 72-game season plus the playoffs—there was just one game left, 48 minutes of combat that would determine who were "Kings of the Cage."

And as little Sid Borgia bounced the ball and signaled the giant centers Kerr and Foust to come into the circle, the jammed throng let go with wild enthusiasm.

But the cheering died abruptly. Fort Wayne, starting with a touch and fury that had not been previously evidenced during the hard-fought series, dashed away to a quick lead. The pivotal figure in this drive was Foust. He scored the first 10 points for the Hoosiers and rebounded so strongly that he prevented Cervi's speedier forces from employing their spectacular fast break. When the Nats began to find the range and closed to within 3 points, Foust began to deal the ball off to teammates Brian and Mel Hutchins, who also hit the mark. So when the two squads took a break at the end of the first period, the torrid-shooting Pistons had a 10-point lead, 31–21. They had shot the eyes out of the hoop, hitting 57 per cent of their shots to only 36 per cent for the Nats.

Houbregs, subbing to give Foust a blow, Andy Phillip and Dick Rosenthal continued to bomb the mark as the second quarter opened, and when Hutchins hit still another one-hander from the corner, Cervi asked for time. It was now 41–24—17 big points—and the red-hot Pistons were making the Nats look like some pick-up team. Old-pro Cervi, one of the more colorful dribblers and playmakers in his day, read the riot act. He called for aggressive defense, then looked to his deep bench and chose Billy Kenville.

The lean, pale youngster began driving for the hoop, and when he wasn't hitting his layups, he was drawing fouls. Ken-

171

ville's spark, together with Schayes' arching rainbows from outside, changed the complexion of the game. So did Fort Wayne's deliberate fouling strategy, which backfired. The Pistons soon got themselves in foul trouble, and when the Nats went on a 14–2 surge, they were right back in business. With only 38 seconds left to the half, Cervi's battlers had closed to within 2 points and the home crowd had come alive. But Brian and Foust hit just before the buzzer to let the Pistons breathe a little easier at halftime, 53–47.

Borgia and fellow referee Lou Eisenstein had no trouble making it to the locker room, for the large crowd was still buzzing about the Nats' breathtaking rally. In the third quarter the Nats kept close until Schayes and Seymour hit on consecutive shots. Now the Nats finally looked the Pistons in the eye—it was 57–57, the first deadlock of the struggle since the early going.

It was moments later—after a Piston basket—when Brian pulled the "rock" of the day. The Southern speedster, in attempting to spike King's jump shot fouled Red Rocha, a defensive tower of strength. When King's shot was ruled good and Rocha quickly followed with a foul shot to make it a 3-point play, the Nats had their first lead of the afternoon. The scoreboard blinked 60–59, and when fiery Frankie spotted it as he took the ball out of bounds, he blew his cool. À la football's famed Charlie Brickley, Brian dropkicked the ball up into the stands. A technical foul was immediately assessed, and poised Paul Seymour stepped to the line and cashed it in.

Here Eckman stepped in and showed his leadership. Sensing that this type of a "break" might trigger a collapse, Charley gathered his forces and implored them to stick with the "game plan." And his Pistons reacted superbly and before the third period was over they had knotted the count at 74-all, thanks to some steady firing by Yardley, Brian and Foust.

Bouncy Earl Lloyd opened the final 12-minute session by converting on the end of a fast break, and when Rocha popped in a one-hander the Nats led, 78–74. The home folks really turned on the steam as though the championship were in hand. Even Nats' owner-GM Danny Biasone, who gave himself the title of assistant coach so that he could sit on the bench, permitted his first smile of the afternoon.

However, Brian steamed back and potted a one-handed jumper, and after Kerr pivoted for one of his own, Foust cut the margin to 80–79 by clicking in a 3-pointer to take the wind out of the Syracuse sails. The Nats then opened it to 3 again as Rocha cooly dropped in a pair of free throws. But after Lloyd and Hutchins exchanged hoops, the Pistons drove to an 86-all tie.

The Hoosiers appeared to have the momentum now, and when Foust continued the onslaught by hitting on one of his patented pivots, the crowd was stilled. That is, all but the 40 or so Piston fans who had made up a special excursion from Indiana.

But the rookie Kerr fought back with a free throw, and after Foust hit another foul, Lloyd knotted it up again at 89–89. It was the fifth tie of the hectic half. Moments later, Schayes fouled Phillip, and the free throw sent the Pistons into the lead, 90–89, with just 2:16 to go. The great Schayes had an opportunity to redeem himself quickly, however, when he got fouled driving for the basket. Dolph could put the Nats in front if he netted both his free throws, and knowing this, he knelt—as was his custom in tight situations—and tied his white shoelaces. Now refreshed, the dark-haired Dolph put his right toe gingerly on the line, eyed the hoop, then, with his patented two-handed set shot, tied up matters. Dolph then sent the Nats' followers into rhapsody by also dropping in his second attempt to put Syracuse into a 91–90 lead.

The clock read just 1:23 to go now, and you could see the faces of the Pistons become rigid and tense. The indefatigable Brian came dribbling up the floor and tried a one-hander from his favorite spot in the corner. But it hit the hoop, then rolled off, and the crowd breathed another sigh of relief.

However, the Nats couldn't control the ball and in the frantic skirmish the great Yardley was fouled. Cries of "Miss it! Miss it!" erupted throughout the bubbling building, but the cool, gaunt old pro defied the throng by deadlocking matters at 91-all.

The Nats brought the ball upcourt with quarterback Seymour working the ball deliberately. Schayes passed up a two-handed set when he got crowded. Kerr finally found Lloyd in the corner and Earl threw up a beauty. The crowd went berserk when it went in—but it popped right back out again and the Pistons got the rebound. Now there were 42 seconds showing on the clock when Eckman called time. The Pistons wanted either Yardley or Foust, their best marksmen, to take the shot from in close, hoping for a 3-point play in the bargain. Meanwhile, Cervi had set his matchups. The rugged Seymour was to dog Phillip. Rocha was to take Yardley. King was to go with Brian on the outside—and Schayes was to help clog the middle.

Soon after play was resumed, the Nats got a big break when Yardley was called for palming the ball. Now there were just 18 seconds remaining, and the Pistons needed the basketball. They decided to foul King, for he'd been having trouble throughout the series with his free throws, missing 8 out of 24. So with 12 seconds left, Brian fouled King, and now it was up to the former Morris Harvey dribbling specialist to make good. With his black hair patted in place, the chunky King placed his feet carefully, bounced the ball a half-dozen times, then sent it up one-handed—straight and true.

George King gets a championship ride from his Syracuse teammates.

BOB JOHNSTON (SYRACUSE POST-STANDARD)

It was now 92–91, and Fort Wayne came thundering up court with a rush. It was obvious that their strategy had been to trade 1 point for 2 and win the game with a last-second hoop. As playmaker Phillip dribbled near the basket, the clever Seymour checked him closely. He even feinted Andy into changing directions as he got in tighter. This was Seymour's way of baiting him into a trap, for Andy was unaware that King had been closing in from the opposite direction. Sensing the opportunity, King struck like lightning, swooping in and stealing the ball from the usually sure-fingered Piston.

Joyously, King dribbled once, possibly twice, before he heard a barking cry from Seymour. "Gimme that ball," ordered the Nats' leader. King obeyed promptly, flipping the ball to Paul before watching the last precious seconds tick off the clock to end the game.

"I'd worked too hard for the championship," said Seymour later, "to let him or anyone else lose it on me. If the Pistons were going to steal that ball back they were going to have to chisel it away from me."

By now pandemonium reigned as the Syracuse fans poured onto the floor and hoisted Cervi and King on their shoulders and paraded them triumphantly.

It was the kind of Easter Parade Syracuse's championship fans will never forget.

16

ERNIE THE KID

Tim Moriarty

•

It was Saturday, March 30, 1946—a day that started with a toothache for Mary Vandeweghe. She could feel the pain in her jaw the moment she awoke that morning and she was fully aware of its cause. It was an impacted wisdom tooth that had given her some trouble earlier in the week, but she had twice postponed a trip to the dentist.

Now there could be no further postponement; the pain was too great. So she telephoned her dentist and was given an emergency appointment for later that day.

As she prepared breakfast in the neat kitchen of her home at 30 Court St. in Oceanside, N.Y., Mary Vandeweghe wasn't

Ernie Vandeweghe (11) has his hands full against 7-foot Bob Kurland (17), the big man from the West.

UPI

too upset over the possibility of losing a tooth. She was more concerned about watching her son Ernie play basketball that night at Madison Square Garden. "I'll make the game no matter what happens to the tooth," she vowed.

The occasion was college basketball's first East–West All-Star game and Mary Vandeweghe wasn't about to miss it. Her son had been named to the East team—a singular honor indeed, for Ernie Vandeweghe was only seventeen years old and a freshman at Colgate University. During his first season as a member of the Maroon varsity, Ernie had been sensational, scoring 293 points and attracting nationwide attention as a potential All-American.

A thin smile played upon the lips of Mary Vandeweghe as she sat there in the family kitchen and recalled her son's first game of organized basketball. It had taken place six years earlier—in 1940. The Oceanside team had reached the twelve-to-fourteen-year division final in the Long Island Catholic Youth Organization playoffs. When the Oceanside youngsters arrived at Mineola for the championship game they discovered that one of their players was missing.

Ernie Vandeweghe, only eleven years old then, had made the trip to Mineola as a sort of team mascot. After watching the undermanned Oceanside team warm up, he asked if he could fill in for the absent boy. The coach approved, found him a uniform but couldn't locate an extra pair of sneakers. Ernie didn't mind. He said he would play in his street shoes. And play he did. Ernie went on to score 8 points and lead the Oceanside team to the CYO championship.

Mary Vandeweghe wasn't at Mineola that day to watch her son's debut, but she missed none of Ernie's other games as he progressed through the CYO leagues and then to Oceanside High School, where he starred in basketball, baseball and football.

180

No one was surprised when, following his graduation from Oceanside High, Ernie showed up at Colgate. He had been offered athletic scholarships from numerous colleges around the nation, but he chose to enroll at the Hamilton, N.Y., school without the benefit of any financial aid. The reason? Well, he was simply following in family footsteps. His father, Ernest Vandeweghe, Sr., had been a star soccer player at Colgate and an uncle, Ken Smith, had captained the Maroon basketball and golf teams.

Ernie's parents saw every game the Colgate basketball team played—at home and on the road—that season of 1945–46. Now they were looking forward to watching their son play in the season's climactic contest—the All-Star game.

So Mary Vandeweghe kept her appointment with her dentist later that day and the bothersome wisdom tooth was extracted, then she rushed to join her husband at Madison Square Garden. The entire left side of her face was swollen and discolored, but she still managed a crooked smile of pride when she saw her son trot onto the court with his East teammates.

Turning to her husband, she said, "My Lord, Van, our Ernie looks like a mere boy among those men." It was no illusion. Even at 6-3, Ernie Vandeweghe was dwarfed by most of his rivals. What's more, both squads were sprinkled with World War II veterans who had only recently resumed their college careers. They were four to eight years older than Vandeweghe.

The West squad was led by two giants—7-foot Bob Kurland of Oklahoma A&M and Don Otten of Bowling Green, only a half-inch shorter than Kurland. Their presence had caused Broadway oddsmakers to install the Westerners as 8-point favorites.

When the spotlight shone on Kurland and Otten during the

pregame introductions, there was a collective moan from the capacity crowd of 18,157. And Mary and Ernest Vandeweghe, Sr., seated in Box 36 in the loge section, also moaned.

Then the rest of the West team, coached by Harold Olsen of Ohio State, was introduced. There was Charlie Black, twenty-four, of Kansas University, a former Air Corps captain who had flown fifty-one photo reconnaissance missions in World War II. And Kenny Sailors, twenty-five, another service returnee, a great playmaker, dribbler and shooter from Wyoming. Rounding out Olsen's West squad were Warren Ajax of Minnesota, Rudy Lawson of Purdue, Leo Klier of Notre Dame, Wilbur Schu of Kentucky, Dave Strack of Michigan and Ray Snyder of Ohio State.

Mary Vandeweghe watched Schu warm up and was overcome by a feeling of compassion for the Kentucky player. A fierce competitor, Schu had played the entire season with braces to protect his previously injured knees. But that wasn't the only protection Schu had for this game. His face was also heavily bandaged. During a practice session earlier in the week, Schu had plunged face-first into a brick wall and required ten stitches.

"That poor fellow," Mary Vandeweghe said, tenderly fingering her own aching jaw. "I hope nobody hits him in the face tonight."

Now it was time to introduce the East All-Stars, coached by Joe Lapchick of St. John's. Frank Mangiapane trotted to center court, followed by his New York University sidekick, Sid Tannenbaum, and the Garden rocked with applause. They were joined by mustachioed Harry Boykoff of St. John's, who hobbled out on a damaged right leg that was as stiff as his upper lip. Next came Ernest Vandeweghe, Jr., who a year before was playing for Oceanside High School and now was about to play with and against college basketball's greatest stars. If he looked slightly scared, who could blame him? Then, as the cheers for this lanky Long Island boy rolled down from the balcony, Mary Vandeweghe stood up, turned to her husband and said, "Van, tooth or no tooth, I wouldn't have missed this for the world." The applause was sustained as Ernie Calverley of Rhode Island State trotted out, followed by Ken Shugart of Navy, Harry Zeller of Pittsburgh, Jimmy Joyce of Temple, Harry Donovan of Muhlenberg and Bob Myers of Dartmouth.

Once the introductions were completed, the game officials —husky Matty Begovich and tomato-faced Pat Kennedy— walked onto the floor. It was time for the opening tap. The assembled reporters seated along the press row watched with interest as Lapchick sent out his starting five. Boykoff had already informed Lapchick that his right leg still bothered him during the warmup, so the East coach sent Zeller out to play center against Kurland. It looked like a sad mismatch; at 6 feet 4 inches poor Zeller would be spotting Kurland 8 inches. Lapchick elected to open with Vandeweghe and Myers in the forecourt, Calverley and Tannenbaum in the backcourt. That put Vandeweghe on the ever-dangerous Sailors and Myers on Lawson. The remaining matchups were Calverley vs. Klier and Tannenbaum vs. Black.

Kurland won the opening tap and the ball went to Sailors. The Wyoming cowboy passed cross-court to Lawson, then took a return pass and fired a one-hander from the top of the key—2 points. The West was off and running.

The strategy Lapchick had devised in the hope of reducing the West's tremendous height advantage was revealed the moment his team brought the ball downcourt for the first time. Zeller, instead of setting up near the basket, moved out to play a high post position, taking Kurland with him. This left Vandeweghe and Myers up front to battle for rebounds.

183

One writer sized up the situation immediately and remarked, "Old Joe's trying to keep Kurland away from the boards, but he'd better do something about stopping Sailors." At this early stage of the game it looked like a tough assignment. Sailors popped in three of his team's first four field goals and the West went on from there to open a 23–18 bulge.

Lapchick now had Joyce alternating with Zeller against Kurland, and the dogged East centers were finding it difficult to keep pace with the big man from Oklahoma. During an East time-out, Lapchick turned to Tannenbaum and said, "Sid, bring that ball down fast and then look for the open man. You can do it."

Tannenbaum reacted quickly to Lapchick's order. He set up one basket by Myers and another by Zeller with clever passes to bring the East even for the first time at 23–23. Now Lapchick was off the bench and shouting, "You can do it, gang, you can do it."

Then, with the West leading, 29–25, Zeller hit on a short one-hander and Mangiapane, Vandeweghe's relief man, added two free throws to produce a 29–29 deadlock at intermission. Kurland had 8 points in the first half, well below his average, although it did top both teams. Zeller and Myers led the East scorers with 6 points each. Vandeweghe had 5.

In the East dressing room, Lapchick's halftime instructions to his players were terse and brief. "Don't let Kurland and Sailors go berserk," he said, "and you can beat those guys. Lots of hustle now. Lots of hustle."

The Easterners showed so much hustle at the start of the second half that even Lapchick blinked his eyes in amazement. They went on an 8–0 splurge to barge ahead, 37–29. Zeller started it with a rebound shot. Vandeweghe dropped in a free throw and Calverley, added a medium-range one-hander.

184

Zeller then passed to Myers for a layup and Vandeweghe contributed another free throw.

Now the Easterners were really rolling—especially Vandeweghe. When he wasn't driving for the basket or setting up plays, the Colgate freshman was battling Kurland and Otten for rebounds at the other end of the court. Mary Vandeweghe and Ernest Vandeweghe, Sr., were finding it hard to control their emotions. During a time-out they moved from the loge section to courtside seats behind the press section. They wanted a closer look at their son in action.

The West, though, wasn't finished yet. Kurland, Strack and Sailors kept hacking away at the East's lead and pulled their team to within 1 point at 52–51 with 6 minutes left to play. Now it was time for Vandeweghe to shine again. His accomplice was the burly Mangiapane. Twice Vandeweghe moved to within shooting position, then passed off to Mangiapane, who clicked both times. A third Mangiapane basket upped the East's lead to 58–51.

After Black converted a rebound for the West, Vandeweghe passed to Tannenbaum and the East's lead was back to 7 points with 2 minutes remaining. The whole Garden now was cheering for Vandeweghe, who had set up three of his team's last four baskets with deft passes. Then the never-say-die Sailors wriggled in for one of his push shots. And after an East turnover, Ajax hit with a set shot to cut the West's deficit to 60–57.

Now there were only 70 seconds remaining and the East was freezing the ball, waiting for an opening. Finally, Donovan pushed up a shot that rolled off into Western hands and was tossed upcourt to Black. The tall Kansan dumped in the layup with 8 seconds left on the clock.

The Westerners went into a full-court press. And it worked.

On the East's pass-in the ball was fumbled and Sailors—the indefatigable Sailors—recovered it and fired a short one-hander. The ball hit the front of the rim, rolled uncertainly for an instant and then fell back into the mob scene under the West basket as the buzzer sounded.

The underdog East had won college basketball's first All-Star Game, 60–59, principally through the efforts of that tall, baby-faced seventeen-year-old, Ernie Vandeweghe. He finished the game with 14 points, tying Sailors for scoring honors. But just as important were the four East baskets he had set up in the last half, including the winning shot by Tannenbaum.

And nobody was surprised when Ernie was called to center court to receive the game's Most Valuable Player trophy. As he posed for the photographers, flanked by his deliriously happy parents, Ernie turned to his mother and asked, "How's that bad tooth, Mom?"

Mary Vandeweghe smiled through her puffed cheeks and said, "What tooth, son?"

17

COUSY'S
OVERTIME PAYOFF

Andy Carra

•

•

Bob Cousy sat on the long green bench in the Boston Garden home-team dressing room. He was dressed in the Boston Celtic warmup suit, with his arms folded across his chest and his feet, neatly wrapped in ankle-high black sneakers, crossed out in front of him. He was the picture of serenity—just the opposite of Celtic coach Arnold ("Red") Auerbach, who was pacing the floor in front of him.

It was March 21, 1953, and the Celtics were just moments away from taking the floor for the second game of the first round of the NBA Eastern Division playoffs. The Celtics had won the first game from the Syracuse Nationals, 87–81, and

Boston's Bob Cousy works his dribbling magic against
Syracuse's Paul Seymour (5) and Red Rocha.   UPI

if they could beat the Nats again they would advance to the second round for the first time in their seven-year history.

Cousy had joined Boston three years before, after graduating from Holy Cross College, a small Catholic school that played many games in this same Boston Garden. He hadn't been drafted by Boston—he had joined the team after Celtic owner Walter Brown picked his name out of a hat. The NBA had been having some financial troubles just prior to the 1950 draft of college players, and Cousy was taken by the Tri-Cities Blackhawks. But because of personnel shifts (Tri-Cities wanted the services of a proven professional instead of a college draftee) the Blackhawks gave up their top draft choice (Cousy) in order to help stock the player pool created when the Chicago franchise folded. Bob had hoped to be drafted by the Celtics and play in the Boston area, but the same Red Auerbach who was now pacing up and down in front of him said he was too small to grab on the first round. When Brown selected Cousy's name out of then-NBA commissioner Maurice Podoloff's hat, Bob couldn't have been happier. Boston was the only place to play.

Even though Auerbach didn't want Cousy, and even though Walter Brown wasn't exactly pleased with his draw, Cousy turned out to be the best bargain the Celtics ever got. In his first year the 6-1 Cousy finished second on the team in scoring with a 15.6 average. Only "Easy Ed" Macauley scored more. Cousy led the team in assists and finished fourth in the league in that department.

The next year he moved up to a 21.7 scoring average, this time leading the Celtics in scoring, and moved up to second in the NBA in assists. And it was in that second year that Bob Cousy became the leader of the team. His dribbling and passing, as well as his scoring, turned the Celtics into steady winners.

The following season he brought the Celtics to a 46–25 won-lost record, the best in their history up to that time. They finished third in the East, only 1½ games behind the first-place New York Knickerbockers, with the Syracuse Nats sandwiched in between. Cousy had a 19.8 scoring average, good enough for third place in the league's scoring race. His assist total of 547 was 150 better than anyone else's.

So the 1952–53 season was a pretty successful one for the Celtics. In addition to Cousy, Boston had two other men in double figures—Ed Macauley (20.3) and Cousy's partner at guard, Bill Sharman (16.2). In team totals, the Celtics finished the year first in scoring in the NBA. Unfortunately, Boston also gave up the third-highest point total. Still it was a good year. And now it could be even better if the Celtics could get past the Nats and make it to the second round of the playoffs.

Syracuse had a solid team. It was good enough to finish in front of Boston in the regular season, and there didn't seem to be any reason why it couldn't beat the Celtics in the playoffs. Dolph Schayes, the Nats' high-scoring forward, was already one of the league's brightest stars. Schayes had averaged nearly 18 points a game during the regular season. Three other players, Paul Seymour, George King and Red Rocha, had also scored in double figures. Only the Celtics had scored more points during the season than Syracuse. The Nats were tough. And Bob Cousy and the rest of the Celts knew that coming off their first-game loss two nights before, the Nats would be tougher than usual.

After 4 minutes of play, Celtic forward Bob Brannum found out how tough the Nats really were. Brannum and Dolph Schayes had been guarding each other throughout the season and were guarding each other extra close in this game. Both were big, strong men and there was bound to be some

191

friction between them. Sure enough a fight broke out. Officials quickly restored order and both players were banished from the court. Out with Brannum went his 6.8 scoring average—but out with Schayes went a 17.8 average. Most of the 11,058 fans thought it was all over when the Syracuse star walked off. But they were in for a surprise.

Despite the loss of Schayes, the Nats hung in there. The score changed hands throughout the game. Into the third and fourth periods the two clubs struggled and tore at each other. Fouls were called frequently. But through it all—the whistles, the pressure, the roughness—Bob Cousy went about his business with his usual flair. But somehow it wasn't quite enough. With only seconds remaining, Cousy had 24 points, but the Nats had a 1-point lead, 77–76. The Nats also had the ball, so the Celtics pressed all over the court. Suddenly there was a crush of bodies around the midcourt line and out of the group came Cousy. He dribbled toward the basket. Then there was a flick of the wrist that fed the ball to a teammate under the basket. But the pass was wild and flew out of bounds, and with it, seemingly, flew Boston's chance to put the clincher on the Nats.

But again the Celtics gained possession of the ball. And naturally they gave it to Cousy, who began dribbling and looking for an opening. The Syracuse players, knowing that Cousy was the one who could hurt them the most, swarmed all over him. A foul was called and Bob was going to the line for one free throw. The scoreboard showed 5 seconds left in the game. Bob stepped to the line, bounced the ball a couple of times, set himself, then softly pushed a one-hander into the air. The ball floated through the net and the game went into overtime.

Through the first overtime period the teams continued their hard-fought struggle. First the Nats would score, then the

Celtics would come back. The teams continued the pace until it came down to almost the exact situation during regulation time—the only difference was that Syracuse now had 86 points and the Celtics 85. Of the 8 points Boston had scored in overtime, Cousy had 5. Now, once again with only seconds remaining, Cousy went to the foul line for one shot. Again he calmly stepped to the line, and again he bounced the ball a couple of times, aimed—and again the ball trickled down through the net to send the game into another extra period.

Strategy changed in the second overtime. Both Syracuse coach Al Cervi and Boston's Auerbach told their teams to take their time and play for the good shot. Syracuse got the first opportunity and big Red Rocha put one in from underneath. Boston came back and put one in, then the Nats scored once more. If there was any pressure shifting from one team to the other, the pressure skipped right over the placid Cousy. With time running out the Celtics got the ball to Cooz. Seconds remained and Boston trailed, 90–88. Cousy began dribbling around, setting up. Suddenly he spotted an opening, drove for the basket. But as quickly as he began his drive, the Syracuse defense closed up like a football line. It was too late to stop Cousy. He took another step, stopped short and let go a one-hander. Swish! Into the third overtime they went.

By now the Nats were getting into serious foul trouble—and to make matters worse, guard Paul Seymour had sprained an ankle and was virtually immobile. But instead of this demoralizing them, the Syracuse players rallied and came up with a super effort. With only 13 seconds left they led 99–94 —despite the presence of only four able-bodied men. If the Syracuse performance was inspirational, it only served to bring out the best in Bob Cousy.

The Celtics got the ball to him and he drove up the court like a madman. In and out of bodies he whirled until he came up to the Syracuse foul line and let go with a shot. As he released the ball, Celtic owner Walter Brown—the man who had picked Cousy's name out of a hat three years before—turned away from the action. He just couldn't bear to watch anymore. Whether he was a victim of pressure or merely a disgruntled owner, no one can say. No matter what he was feeling at the moment, he never did get to see Cousy's shot fall through, closing the Nats' lead to 3 points. He did hear the referee's whistle—signaling the 49th foul against Syracuse. Once again Bob Cousy stepped to the free-throw line, and once again he did what came naturally—bounce, bounce, bounce, aim. His body set in that strangely calm-looking pose of a man waiting for a bus, hips twitched, Bob softly arched his shot up and in. It was now 99–97.

As the shot went through, there were 5 seconds showing on the clock—time for one more minor miracle? Sure enough, the Celtics got it—thanks to their own aggressiveness. The Nats' pass-in went deep into Boston territory and after a series of deflections went straight to Cousy. Bob headed in a direct line for the basket. Seeing that time was about to run out just after he crossed the midcourt line, Cousy let go with a half-hook and half-push shot. As the ball traveled through the air the Boston Garden buzzer warned that unless it went in the game was over. The buzzer was still sounding when the ball burst through the net, tying the game, 99–99. Cousy had tied the second game of the playoffs for the fourth time. In the third overtime Boston had scored 9 points, 8 by Cousy. Each time the Nationals had seemingly wrapped the game up, Cousy had come back and single-handedly wiped out the lead.

But if the men from Syracuse were giving up in the face of what seemed like a home-town miracle, they didn't show it. The Nats had to give away a technical foul shot every time a personal foul was called against them, since they had run out of legal substitutions, and every time a man over the foul limit committed a foul the Celtics were awarded an extra shot. Despite the need to avoid fouls and despite the fact that they were playing with four mobile men and Paul Seymour, the Nationals ripped off 5 straight points at the start of the fourth overtime period.

Boston didn't give up, either. With Cousy guiding them, the Celtics slowly closed the gap and gained control of the game. The lead was down to 3, then 2. When Cousy scored a basket on a one-hander, publicity director Howie McHugh fainted. The tension had gotten to him, finally, just as the Celtics tied it up, 105–105. McHugh missed the best part. Boston didn't stop there. The Celtics scored 6 more points and wound up outscoring Syracuse 12–6 in the fourth overtime to win the game, 111–105. Cousy had scored 9 of the Boston points in that period.

It was a fantastic performance and made all the more formidable by the fact that it came in the pressure-packed playoffs. Cousy had scored 50 points in the game, splitting his total evenly between regulation time and overtime. Twenty-five points in four overtime periods! There has never been an overtime performance to equal Cousy's.

195

18

NIGHT
OF THE HAWK

John J. Archibald

•

•

Have you ever heard 10,000 people booing at the same time?

If so, you know a man wouldn't exactly have to strain to capture the delicate tones. But that's what Boston Celtics coach Red Auerbach pretended to be doing the night of April 12, 1958, after his introduction to the crowd jammed into cozy little Kiel Auditorium in St. Louis. Auerbach grinned broadly and taunted the fans by cupping his hand around his ear, as though to magnify the ovation.

Red knew the crowd was particularly anxious to get on him this night, because the fans felt their St. Louis Hawks were going to give Auerbach and his Celtics a long-overdue shellacking. It was Game No. 6 of the NBA championship series.

199

St. Louis' Bob Pettit maneuvers against Boston's Bill Russell. UPI

The Hawks led, 3 victories to 2, and they could bring St. Louis its first title by winning one more.

The Hawk partisans were optimistic because the man the Boston defense—and offense—was built around, Bill Russell, was sidelined with a leg injury. Russell was hurt in the third quarter of Game No. 3 and had sat out the next two contests. Ed Macauley, a 6-8 forward who had played six seasons with the Celtics and was in his second campaign as a Hawk, recalled, "For us, the sixth game was the final. There were reports that Russell might play in this one. Certainly it seemed likely that he'd be ready to go if there were a seventh game two nights later in Boston. We'd never beaten the Celtics there in a title game."

Macauley's reasoning seemed sound, even though coach Alex Hannum's St. Louisans had won the opening game of the series in Boston, 104–102, with a healthy Russell in the pivot. The Celtics had come back to demolish the Hawks the following night. When the series moved to St. Louis the Hawks won Game No. 3 by 3 points, with Russell on the bench throughout the final quarter. Russell fell while blocking a shot, suffering what later was diagnosed as pulled ankle tendons and a bone chip in his right leg.

The Celtics shocked St. Louis to its core, however, by beating the Hawks, 109–98, in Kiel Auditorium two nights later —without Russell. The Hawks then gained their 3–2 advantage with a 102–100 victory in Boston, as Bob Pettit drilled in 33 points.

And now it was Game No. 6.

"We tried to be nonchalant before the game," said Macauley, who had been a hero dozens of times on this same court while gaining All-America status with St. Louis University. "But the attempts at casual conversation had a phony ring. We were tense."

So was Hannum. The season before, his first as a coach after a so-so playing career in the NBA, Alex had directed the Hawks to a Western Division title and playoff crown but couldn't quite get by the Celtics in the championship series. Boston won the seventh game, 125–123, in double overtime.

The Hawks did equally well in the regular season of 1957–58, but the volatile Hannum and the team's flamboyant owner, Ben Kerner, had a couple of highly publicized differences. There was little doubt that if he lost again to Boston, Hannum would join Kerner's scrap pile of coaches. In the dressing room, however, Hannum stuck to his pattern of avoiding any pregame pep talk. Charley Share, the Hawks' massive center and captain, said that as a coach Hannum's only vocal effort at firing up the club was a shout—if on the road—of "Red ball!"

"We wore red on the road and that would be the referee's call if we had earned possession of the ball," Share explained. "If a ball was loose or if it was coming off the backboard, the Hawks knew they were supposed to get it, by whatever means were necessary. Red ball, or else."

The battlecry was "White ball!" in Game No. 6, with the Hawks wearing their basically white home uniforms, and it was echoed frequently by the officials as Hannum's men crashed brutally under the boards. Russell was in uniform when the game began, but on the bench. It wasn't surprising, because just the day before Auerbach had said, "We miss Russell, but we don't want to subject him to the risk of permanent injury." But now the risk was apparently forgotten, however, for with 6:14 remaining in the initial quarter, Russell half-limped, half-trotted onto the court. Boston led the tight Hawks, 7–4, at the time. It appeared that Auerbach was sending in Russell as a psychological blow—a crusher.

Russell got an appreciative hand from the crowd. He got a

201

series of hips and elbows from the Hawks, who were in no mood to play Help the Handicapped. Bob Pettit, the former LSU great then in his fourth season as a pro, began connecting on jump shots and on second-effort attempts in the melees under the hoop. Russell couldn't contain him and Pettit scored a dozen points before the period ended with St. Louis in front, 22–18.

Boston's attack depended largely upon superguard Bob Cousy, particularly with Russell unable to rebound and fire the ball downcourt with his usual sharpness. Cousy was hounded, however, by an NBA veteran the Hawks had obtained specifically to deal with him, Slater ("Dugie") Martin. Martin, matching Cousy in tricks if not fancy footwork, made every shot a tough one for Bob. In the first half, Cousy totaled just 2 points. St. Louis outscored the Celtics in the second period, 35–34, and had a 5-point lead at the half. Pettit had added 9 points in the quarter for a total of 21. Russell, trying desperately to hinder Pettit but lacking the agility because of his painful ankle, committed his fourth personal foul before the half ended and had to be benched by Auerbach.

The capacity Kiel Auditorium crowd exploded as the Hawks returned to the floor for the second half. It was more than just the possibility of a championship that excited the spectators. It was the chance of wiping the grin from the face of Auerbach, the master villain. The St. Louisans remembered a game in the previous year's playoffs, for instance, when Auerbach infuriated the Hawks by insisting before the opening buzzer that the baskets did not seem to be at regulation height. Red demanded that he be allowed to measure the distance from floor to rim and went on the court with a steel measuring rule to do so. Ben Kerner blew his top at this and charged from his seat at courtside—from an area called "Murderers' Row" because of the referee-baiting conducted there by Kerner and a group of rabid cohorts—and demanded that Auerbach get the hell off the floor. Auerbach responded by taking a swing at Kerner, with most of the force wasted in the smoke-filled air. Players, police and fans separated the two men, but the Boston leader's attempt to kayo the popular owner added to the fans' hatred of Red for years to come.

The Celtics' owner, Walter Brown, further incited St. Louis just before the 1958 playoffs began by saying, "The Celtics are as strong in the stronger Eastern Division as the Hawks are weak in the weaker Western Division." "Alex Hannum," Brown told the press, "is a basketball accident, a man with very little coaching ability."

For such reasons the St. Louis fans remained in near pandemonium during the second half as they saw the Celtics threaten to deprive them of this chance for revenge. For the Celts battled back. Not right away, as the hot-shooting Pettit made his team's first 6 points at the start of the third quarter. Cliff Hagan, the spectacular 6-4 Kentuckian at the other corner for St. Louis, also began sliding through to score on hook shots. Hagan had outshone Pettit in the earlier games of the playoffs, popping in 136 points in five contests.

After St. Louis pulled to a 10-point lead midway in the third quarter, the Celtics began to come on. Tommy Heinsohn started hitting from the corners. So did Frank Ramsey and Lou Tsioropoulos and Bill Sharman. And Cousy. The Cooz, flicking the ball behind his back for basket-producing passes, flinging the ball into the net himself on fast breaks, sinking short jumpers, started making the Hawk fans sweat. Cousy scored 7 points in one stretch of less than 3 minutes, but at the end of the period St. Louis still led, 83–77.

The green-uniformed visitors tied the score at 84–84, though, and it was clearly anybody's game. Again and again the lead switched as Boston employed a variety of gunners while St. Louis seemed to have but one thought: Get the ball to Pettit.

"We felt that if we shot and missed, we were losing 2 points," said Macauley, "because Bobby could put it in."

The funnel to Pettit frequently was Share, 6-10 and 260 pounds, who enjoyed being an immovable shield for Pettit's jump shots. Charley was proud of his role.

"Hannum had a knack of building pride in each individual on the team," said Share. "My skills were admittedly limited, but Alex explained to me that my function was to get the rebounds, play good defense and set picks for Pettit. And, yes, because I was pretty rugged, I guess you could say I also was 'the hatchet man.' If any rough stuff was needed, that is."

As the final minutes ticked off, Pettit made as frequent use of Share as possible, but often it was necessary for Bob to slam his way in under the basket and shoot as best he could. He barely beat the 24-second clock with a short jumper that made it 100–95 in favor of St. Louis. Minutes later he exceeded George Mikan's record of 42 points for a championship playoff game with a basket that gave him 44 and the Hawks a 103–98 lead. Then two free throws by Pettit made it 105–100 at the 2-minute mark.

Cousy, who had been bottled up again by Dugie Martin after his third-quarter splurge, sank a field goal from outside and then made two free throws to reduce the margin to 105–104. Free throws by Heinsohn and the Hawks' Win Wilfong offset each other, but then Pettit found an opening and drove through for a layup and it was 108–105.

Heinsohn connected twice from the charity stripe to trim the St. Louis lead to a point. When the Hawks got the ball, they called time with 36 seconds remaining.

"The plan," Share said, "was to let Martin shoot the basket, because we knew Pettit would be surrounded. Everybody was to crash the boards when he shot, though, in case Dugie missed."

Martin's shot bounced off the rim, and it was Pettit who got the rebound. Share said, "I saw Bobby do something then that he had trained himself for long before. He believed that many big men get into difficulty because after they get a rebound they bring the ball down so they can jump high for their shot. Many times a shorter man can tie up the rebounder before he gets his shot away. Pettit, instead, sacrificed some of his jump for surprise, by letting the ball go toward the hoop as soon as he got control. That's what he did with 16 seconds left that night and the basket he got brought us the championship."

Pettit's goal gave the Hawks a 3-point lead and made his total 50. The St. Louisans were very careful not to foul Sharman as he sped in for a basket at the other end of the court that provided the final score: Hawks, 110; Celtics, 109.

Macauley had possession of the ball as the Hawks fought their way upcourt, and when the game-ending buzzer sounded he fired the ball toward the Kiel roof. Share eluded the crowd that surged onto the court, grabbed the ball and muscled his way to the dressing room with it. "I knocked over my wife, Rose, as I went through the crowd," said Share. "She's never let me forget it."

The Hawk fans had their moment of triumph over Auerbach, and Hannum had his hour of glory—not much more than an hour, however, for Hannum and Kerner couldn't reach an agreement on a contract for the following season and Alex was turned loose. In the seasons that followed, Hannum, as an opposing coach, was the target of the booing thousands in St. Louis. But these were not the same quality jeers that were reserved for Red Auerbach, the villain whom Hannum and his Hawks had upended on that April night in 1958.

205

19

THE BLITZ KIDS

Joe Gergen

•

·

Vadal Peterson stood disconsolately in a dressing room under the stands at Madison Square Garden. He had brought his Utah team 2,269 miles for its first taste of national glory and he was about to lead them back to Salt Lake City with only the taste of ashes.

"The kids were a little tight playing here for the first time, a little gawky-eyed at all the people," Peterson said. "They're a young bunch. They only average eighteen years. I wish we could play here again."

But, of course, the Utes could not. At least not this season. They had lost to Kentucky, 46–38, in their first NIT appear-

Utah's Arnie Ferrin led the Blitz Kids into Madison Square Garden.   UPI

ance. This mystery team from what seemed to New Yorkers a foreign land had captivated the crowd with its spirit and exciting brand of play, but all for naught. The heartsick Utah players went back to their hotel rooms and began to pack for the long train ride home. It was the night of March 20, 1944.

NCAA officials wanted Utah to appear in its Western regional tournament at Kansas City, Missouri. But when the NCAA refused to guarantee Utah's expenses, Peterson balked. Shortly thereafter, the Utah coach received a call from New York.

"We need an eighth team to complete the National Invitation roster," tournament director Ned Irish said. "It'll be a tough field for your kids, but we thought maybe . . ."

Irish never got to finish his sentence. "Mister," Peterson interrupted, "we'll come anywhere that we can get a decent game."

And so while New York writers explained to their readers that basketball was indeed played in Utah, Peterson herded his players into a train. Only one member, Fred Sheffield, the 6-1 center who was prepared to meet Kentucky's Bob Brannum, Bowling Green's 6-11 Don Otten and giant George Mikan of DePaul, had ever seen New York. Sheffield had leaped 6 feet 8 inches to win the NCAA high-jump championship the previous spring and had earned the right to appear in the Amateur Athletic Union championships at New York, where he finished third.

The combination of the long train ride, the big city and Kentucky was just too much for the Utes to handle. Despite a brilliant performance by Arnie Ferrin, who scored 13 points, intercepted countless passes and rebounded superbly, Utah's cold-shooting second half was costly.

Midway between the packing of the shirts and socks, the

phone rang in Peterson's room. The call was from Kansas City; the NCAA officials were in a dither. Arkansas, one of the four teams slated to play in the Western regionals, had withdrawn after two of its leading players were seriously injured in an automobile accident. Utah was asked to substitute, and the Utes agreed, after Peterson had been assured that his financial demands would be met. The Utes were jubilant at the sudden opportunity. "We'll be back here in a week," Ferrin said, "to play the Eastern NCAA champ."

And so the Utes set out for Kansas City. The trip required two and a half days due to the erratic train schedules caused by moving wartime troops. By the time Utah faced Missouri on Friday night, March 24, St. John's had already reached the NIT finals by upsetting Bowling Green and stunning Kentucky. Utah made history that night without firing a shot. The Utes became the first team to participate in both the NIT and NCAA competitions in the same season. Not content with this, they went out and romped to a 45–35 victory as Ferrin scored 12 points and dazzled Missouri with his speed and aggressiveness.

Iowa State, which had defeated Pepperdine in the other Western semifinal game, was better prepared. The Cyclones double-teamed Ferrin and held him to 6 points. But Sheffield and little Wat Misaka scored 9 each and led Utah to an easy 40–31 triumph, one which fulfilled Ferrin's promise and sent the Utes back to New York to meet Eastern champion Dartmouth for the NCAA title.

The following night, while the Western upstarts lurched by rail toward New York once again, St. John's made a little history of its own. The Redmen defeated DePaul, 47–39, and won an unprecedented second consecutive NIT title. St. John's sat back and awaited the outcome of the NCAA final.

St. John's would meet the Dartmouth–Utah winner in a special Red Cross benefit pairing the NIT and NCAA champions. On the eve of the NCAA final, however, it was announced by the Department of the Navy that Dartmouth would under no condition be permitted to play the Red Cross game. The majority of the Dartmouth team, including stars Dick McGuire and Bob Gale, were Navy and Marine Corps trainees stationed at Hanover under the wartime Navy V-12 program. Dartmouth had orders to go back to school after the NCAA final.

It was a bitter blow to the Red Cross. It meant Utah, win or lose, would face St. John's, and almost everyone agreed the Utes would lose to Dartmouth's heavily favored veterans. Thus the Red Cross game would be anticlimactic.

There was at least one interested party, however, who didn't believe Dartmouth was a sure thing. At 6 A.M. on the day of the game, Peterson was awakened in his hotel room by a sharp knock on the door.

"What is it?" he asked, poking his head into the hall.

"Peterson, coach of Utah?" inquired a large figure bundled in an overcoat, his face shielded by a turned-down hatbrim.

"Yes," Peterson said.

"What'll it take to arrange for Dartmouth to win by 12 or more tonight?" the figure asked.

The response from Peterson, normally the most mild-mannered of coaches, burnt the toast in the coffee shop some ten floors below. The intruder retreated.

And Peterson's team was no less magnificent that night. Peterson had devised a gambling defense that he called a "pickup" to shut off the high-scoring Gale and big Aud Brindley, who had posted a new NCAA playoff mark of fourteen field goals in a 60–53 victory over Ohio State. The maneuver enabled Utah to alternately double-team the Indians' big men,

212

leaving an open man somewhere on the floor—but Dartmouth was never to find him.

The two teams battled on even terms throughout most of the game until Utah opened a 36–32 lead with a minute remaining. But Gale tapped in a rebound to cut the deficit to 2 points and, with 3 seconds remaining, McGuire—who had begun the season at St. John's—made a set shot to send the game into overtime.

Ferrin, on the verge of exhaustion, kept Utah even in the extra period, pushing his total to 22 as the teams deadlocked at 40-all. As the final seconds ticked off, Herb Wilkinson worked himself loose, behind the free-throw circle and arched a one-hander toward the basket. The ball hung on the back of the rim for an instant, then dropped in. Utah had won, 42–40.

Bring on St. John's.

Ten nights later, 18,125 fans filled the Garden to watch Utah and St. John's clash for the national championship of basketball. Now the Utes were no longer mystery men when they came on the court for their pregame warmups. Even the patrons in the uppermost reaches of the second balcony knew the identity of Arnie Ferrin, Fred Sheffield, Herb Wilkinson and Wat Misaka, the squat guard whose lineage traced from Japan to Hawaii to the Great Salt Lake. They were the Blitz Kids now, a team of stringy one-handed shooters who ran until they could run no more, a team that had fought against overwhelming odds just to be here. The reception they received from the crowd was warm and even challenged the ovation accorded the local favorites, St. John's, the NIT champions.

As he sat on the bench awaiting the start of his team's most important game—a wartime benefit that would earn

$35,000 for the Red Cross—Peterson couldn't help but wonder at the turn of events that had placed him and his band of home-grown Mormon youngsters where they were.

Utah had begun the season without a home court thanks to the Army, which had appropriated the field house, so Peterson moved the team into a church gym. Then there was the matter of opponents. The Skyline Conference, of which Utah was a member, had suspended play because of the war, so the Utes scratched and scrounged for opponents. It was said that their biggest task was not beating college opponents but finding them. The Utes found only two, Weber State and Colorado, and beat them both. The other 16 victories and 3 defeats that dotted the Utah schedule were accomplished with the aid of service and industrial teams, many of which boasted former college stars and all of which held a big advantage in experience. Utah's best player, in fact, was a freshman, a 6-3½ collection of bones connected to bright red cheeks and a hank of blond hair, Arnie Ferrin. Peterson knew he had something special the first day he saw Ferrin, a great-grandson of a pioneer who trudged across the plains with Brigham Young to found Salt Lake City in 1847.

The piercing sound of the warning buzzer jarred Peterson back to the present. Now his team would try to complete one of the most amazing comebacks in sports history. Joe Lapchick, the resourceful St. John's coach, sent Ivy Summer out to jump center against Sheffield, who was hampered by an ankle injury suffered in the Dartmouth game. The Redmen from Brooklyn were favored by 4 points.

St. John's got the opening tap and the Redmen's Bill Kotsores quickly broke in alone for a layup. But he missed. St. John's passing game was something, but the Johnnies' shooting was something else. The Redmen baffled the Utah defense throughout the first 7 minutes, but fluffed nine layups. Ferrin

214

scored his team's first 7 points, but still the Utes trailed, 9–7. And Sheffield limped to the sidelines a minute later, replaced by Misaka.

St. John's moved to a 13–8 lead, but Utah gamely fought back. Ferrin provided the inspiration and the playmaking, setting up Wilkinson and Bob Lewis for baskets, while Misaka hounded the St. John's ballhandlers. When the first-half buzzer sounded, Utah had pulled even, 19–19, and the crowd was in a frenzy.

The sentimental battle was just about over. The Garden crowd had adopted Utah. The clean-cut Blitz Kids had turned on the fans like few sports aggregations ever had. When the Utes came onto the court for the start of the second half, they were greeted with a deafening ovation. But the battle for prestige and honor was just beginning. Buoyed by the ovation, Utah ran off 5 straight points as Ferrin dominated both ends of the court. Then the cool Redmen came back to tie.

Suddenly the Blitz Kids cut loose. They rattled off 9 consecutive points with a dazzling exhibition of speed and shooting prowess. It was 35–26 in their favor with 11 minutes remaining. But St. John's wasn't through.

Slowly, ever so slowly, they chopped down the lead. Three baskets by Ray Wertis and a Summer hook shot lifted the Redmen to within 2 points with 5 minutes remaining. The crowd came alive with excitement once again.

Then Ferrin stole the ball and passed to Wilkinson, who tossed in a one-hander. Seconds later, Ferrin leaped high to grab a rebound and dribbled the entire length of the court. He made a twisting move for the basket and, with two St. John's players hanging on him, scored his first field goal in 20 minutes. He completed a 3-point play by sinking his free throw.

Ferrin, fittingly, capped the night when he again raced from

Utah's Bob Lewis (31) and Wat Misaka (21) try fingertip control against St. John's.   UPI

basket to basket to cap a 17-point performance. The victory, as well as the crowd, belonged to Utah. The Blitz Kids had won, 43–36.

Now they could go back to their hotel rooms and pack their bags with enthusiasm. They had everything they had come to New York to get. And a lot more.

20

McGUIRE'S
YANKEE REBELS

Steve Guback

•

●

It started with some laughter from the first few rows. Then, gradually, the noise grew into one general swell of excitement as more and more people became aware of what was happening on the court. Little blacksmith-shouldered Tommy Kearns of North Carolina, at 5-11, was moving out to jump center against 7-foot-stringbean Wilt Chamberlain of the University of Kansas. It seemed utterly ridiculous.

"Hey, McGuire," came a call from the Kansas rooting section, "you giving up already?"

Frank McGuire, the North Carolina coach, gripped a towel

221

Long-armed Lennie Rosenbluth of North Carolina defenses Kansas' Wilt Chamberlain in NCAA championship game. UPI and sat hunched on the Tar Heels' bench. He had been wrestling with a problem while he turned and tossed in his sleep the previous night. How do you cope with a 7-footer? A giant named Chamberlain? And that's what 10,500 fans at Kansas Municipal Auditorium wanted to know. Millions more across the country were tuned in to their radios that night of March 23, 1957, waiting for the answer.

It would be a long, long wait. North Carolina and Kansas would battle through the longest NCAA championship game on record. It would end at 12:14 A.M., Chapel Hill, North Carolina, time.

The setting could hardly have been more dramatic. On one side there was Kansas' Chamberlain—Wondrous Wilt, Wilt the Stilt. He had been the most highly sought-after athlete in the history of the sport ever since his sophomore days at Philadelphia's Overbrook High. By the time he was an eighteen-year-old high school senior, Wilt had offers from more than 100 colleges. Even the Harlem Globetrotters and the NBA had joined in the bidding.

Wilt was 7 feet tall, but he had more than height to recommend him. He could run a quarter-mile in 49 seconds and put the 16-pound shot 48 feet. While competing on Kansas' track team that spring, he won the Big Seven high jump with a leap of 6 feet 5 inches.

On the other side was North Carolina's Lennie Rosenbluth, a lean, lithe shooter with a jewel thief's eye. He had every shot in the book and fantastic accuracy. In 26 of North Carolina's 31 games he had been his club's leading scorer. He held virtually all of UNC's scoring records, including the single-game high of 47 points. Many considered him the best shooter in college basketball.

It was more than Chamberlain vs. Rosenbluth, though. There was Frank McGuire, a dapper, smiling forty-two-year-old Irishman. He was a New Yorker through and through—his mannerisms, his flair for elegant attire. He had been lured to North Carolina four years earlier, after his St. John's team had gone all the way to the NCAA finals only to lose to—you guessed it—Kansas.

Now with a starting five of all New York-area lads, McGuire wanted revenge, and a bit more than that. For the first time since 1949 the nation's No. 1 and No. 2 teams were meeting in an NCAA final, face to face, to decide for themselves who was No. 1. Kansas, a solid, veteran club with a 24–2 record, was in its first year under square-jawed coach Dick Harp. The Jayhawks, No. 2 in the polls, were favored by 3 points. Surprising? Not really. The oddsmakers thought that much of Chamberlain, the towering giant with the unstoppable stuff-shot. But the point spread was clearly an insult to North Carolina, ranked No. 1. Some said the Tar Heels had been lucky. They bristled at that. They were voted No. 1 in mid-January when Kansas was a 2-point upset victim of Iowa State in one of those painful slow-down games. North Carolina stayed atop the polls the rest of the year simply because it stayed undefeated. The Tar Heels won 31 straight, an NCAA record. A half-dozen were excruciatingly close. Three were won in overtime. How's that for luck?

Maybe, too, the oddsmakers felt the law of averages would catch up with North Carolina. That afternoon the lobby of the Muehlebach Hotel, tournament headquarters, was astir with coaches from all over the country. Some said Kansas would win in a rout, some expected a close Kansas victory. North Carolina supporters were as scarce as kind words for referees. No team had ever won 32 straight games in a single season—and North Carolina didn't exactly seem suited for the task. Everybody conceded that the Tar Heels had a crack starting team, but they had little bench.

223

In the Friday night semifinals, Kansas—with Chamberlain repeatedly dunking the ball—crushed San Francisco, 80–56. Meanwhile, the Tar Heels came within a breath of defeat. They had to weather three overtimes before nipping Michigan State. Rosenbluth had pulled that one out heroically, twice stealing the ball for layups in the third overtime period. But the Tar Heels had to be tired, maybe dead-tired. And this was only an average North Carolina team—physically, that is. Joe Quigg, the center, was 6-9. Forwards Pete Brennan and Rosenbluth were 6-6 and 6-5. One guard, Bob Cunningham, was 6-4, and the other, Kearns, was 5-11. They had no one physically intimidating like Wilt the Stilt, who could reach within 6 inches of the basket standing flatfooted and cover 13 feet with a single stride.

"The big guy frightens you, the things he can do with the ball," McGuire told reporters before the game.

It was an honest appraisal, but McGuire had a hunch. He wouldn't try to cope with Wilt at first. He'd ridicule his height and then try to confuse him. That's why he had sent Kearns out for the opening tap. And the crowd reaction was as expected—the laugh. Even the astonished Chamberlain struggled hard against a grin. Wilt controlled the tap, but North Carolina, with its size elsewhere, got the ball back.

"Well, at least that worked," McGuire muttered under his breath.

Kansas, on defense, quickly went into a four-man zone with Chamberlain under the basket to block the close shots and grab the rebounds. The fifth man was man-to-man on Rosenbluth, the Tar Heels' scoring machine. North Carolina worked the ball carefully, and with 56 seconds gone, Rosenbluth cut for the basket off a screen and was fouled. He sank both free throws.

So this was North Carolina's offensive plan. Get the ball

to Rosenbluth. There wasn't any doubt in anybody's mind. Who could blame McGuire if he played it that way? Go with your best weapon, they always say. And Rosenbluth was clearly the Tar Heels' ace. He entered averaging 28.1 points a game, just shy of Chamberlain's 29.6.

What the crowd saw next was Joe Quigg, North Carolina's center, move out to the corner, hoping to draw Chamberlain away from the basket. Wilt didn't budge. So Quigg, the big junior with a baby face, took the initiative, arching in a long one-hander for a 4–0 North Carolina lead.

Quigg, who was only the fourth-best North Carolina scorer that year, scored again from the side. Then Brennan hit a basket and a free throw and North Carolina led, 9–2.

It wasn't until 4:48 had been played that Chamberlain finally scored his first points for the Jayhawks. Now the Kansas rooters felt better. But not for long. Brennan and Quigg continued to hit from the side. Wouldn't they ever miss? North Carolina's lead zoomed to 19–7 and Kansas signaled for a time-out.

Something had to be done to stop the Tar Heels' deadly outside shooting. Harp ordered a man-to-man defense.

Maybe McGuire said a prayer of thanks at that precise time. Quigg moved to the corner again and this time Chamberlain went with him. That was exactly what the Tar Heels wanted. It was more like an ordinary basketball game now, with Wilt's 7-foot height being neutralized as he went outside. McGuire's next move was a honey. He sent Rosenbluth, with his spidery moves and his velvet touch, inside. Rosenbluth missed only twice in the first half and was high man with 14 points. At the halftime buzzer, North Carolina led, 29–22. The Tar Heels' shooting percentage was 64.7 to Kansas' 27.3.

North Carolina had shot well all season, 43.1 per cent, in fact. But 64.7 per cent? They had to start missing, of course.

That's what Harp, still confident, told his Jayhawks in the dressing room.

"Don't panic. Play your game. We'll catch them," Harp said.

He was right. With less than 4 minutes gone in the second half, Kansas moved ahead for the first time. Moments later the Jayhawks had a 5-point lead, and now it was McGuire who called time.

"We've got to slow down, make every shot count," he said. "Take only the shots you know you can make."

The second half was almost like the first, except that Kansas' shooting percentage went up a few points and N.C.'s came down—Rosenbluth, who had been tossing up the softest baskets imaginable, fouled out. When Rosenbluth left with 1:45 to play, North Carolina trailed, 44–43. He had 20 points, the Tar Heels' high, on 8-for-15 from the floor. It was a staggering blow, but Quigg scored on a field goal and Kearns a free throw and North Carolina managed to tie, 46–46, at the end of regulation time.

For the first time in NCAA history, a championship game would go into overtime. A whole new ballgame, but not quite. In addition to losing Rosenbluth on fouls, Quigg, the man who had to guard Chamberlain, had four personal fouls, one short of disqualification.

The crowd sensed something dramatic, maybe a sudden break that would decide it. Bob Young, a senior who had made only eleven field goals all season, replaced Rosenbluth. Maybe Kansas ignored him. If so, it was a costly mistake. Young suddenly broke down the lane and scored a driving layup. Now Kansas had to come back. It got the ball to Chamberlain and Wilt threw in a two-handed jumper from the post, a long-range shot for him. It was 48–48.

North Carolina played for the last shot, but it was Kansas

that wound up getting it. As Brennan was trying to dribble out the clock, Ronnie Loneski, the Jayhawk's senior guard, moved in smartly and forced a jump. Kansas controlled the tap. As the crowd sucked its breath, Loneski took the shot. It missed.

Now a second overtime. Both teams played for one perfect shot, and it was almost like a stall. At one point, Chamberlain and Brennan wrestled for a loose ball and had to be pulled apart. McGuire rushed from the North Carolina bench and Harp jumped to his feet. Players exploded from both benches. Tournament officials and police rushed to the court, finally restoring order amid the milling throng. Neither team scored, but what a tense period it was.

The third overtime period opened—and what was it that Tommy Kearns had said the night before? "We're a chilly club. We play it chilly all the time. I mean we just keep cool. Chamberlain won't give us the jitters like he did to all those clubs."

Kearns was cool, all right. He opened the third overtime period with a field goal from the side and then followed with two free throws to make it 52–48. The North Carolina rooters, featuring cheerleaders in blue and white, went wild. Now the logjam was broken and Kansas threw caution to the wind. Chamberlain got the ball under the hoop. With his tremendous strength he muscled his way up, made his shot and was fouled. Wilt made the free throw to raise his point total to 23 and Kansas now trailed by 1, 52–51.

There was 2:33 left in the third overtime when Maurice King, Kansas' All-Big Seven guard, went to the line for two free throws. He sank his first, missed his second: 52–52.

McGuire cupped his hands and called from the bench, "Play for the last shot!"

North Carolina started its stall. The clock ticked away a

minute, and almost a second one, when suddenly John Parker, Kansas' 6-foot guard, whipped around Quigg and stole the ball. McGuire smashed his fist into his hand. Now the crowd was on its feet. The chesty little Kearns, a bandit who likes to steal the ball, took a desperate lunge at Kansas' Gene Elstun and knocked him almost to the floor. Referee Gene Conway signaled a deliberate foul.

The North Carolina rooters hooted and paper fluttered to the floor, but still Elstun had two free throws coming. And he was one of Kansas' better shooters, team co-captain and No. 13 scorer in the Big Seven the year before. He missed the first but sank the next. Kansas was now on top, 53–52, and 31 seconds were left.

Kearns now took matters into his own hands. He drove for the basket and twisted up acrobatically, but Chamberlain, with his giant wingspan, blocked the shot. Quigg, the trailer on the play, tried to follow up the shot and a whistle sounded on the play.

Foul. Quigg had two shots coming with 6 seconds left. McGuire called a time-out and the team huddled around him on the bench. When it was over Quigg walked to the free-throw line, his hands wet. He bounced the ball nervously. Then he tossed up his first shot, a two-hander, and it went in: 53–53.

One more to go. Quigg's face had a pained expression. For a big man he was a crack free-throw shooter, second best on the team. He bounced the ball again, eyed the rim. Then carefully he put it up and in. The crowd exploded.

North Carolina had it won now, 54–53. But wait. Kansas called time. The crowd pushed down out of the stands and rimmed the playing court. Kansas had time for one desperate scoring play.

Five seconds were left. Kansas put the ball in play and

228

Elstun arched a long, high pass to Chamberlain. Wilt, all 7 feet, jumped up, arms outstretched. But Quigg was also there and with one outstretched hand batted the ball away. Kearns, the little guy, grabbed it and with a happy motion heaved it high into the air. The buzzer sounded.

In Chapel Hill, the instant the game was over, crowds surged everywhere on to the street. Frank McGuire's "Yankee Rebels"—the North Carolinians from up North who had captured the South—had conquered the entire nation.

That 32–0 record. Six overtime periods in two nights. Somehow it didn't seem real. Jack had climbed the beanstalk and toppled the giant. Just like the storybook always said.

21

THE MIRACLE
OF THE KNICKS

Jim O'Brien

•

•

Bill Bradley seems reluctant to overindulge in self-conscious-
ness or to give himself away, but he admits that as a schoolboy in Crystal City, Missouri, he kept a scrapbook devoted
entirely to Wilt Chamberlain. In it he pasted all the pictures
and newspaper clippings he could come up with of Wilt, who
was then a college star at Kansas. And at the same starstruck
age, in the privacy of an empty gymnasium, Bill would let the
ball roll off his fingertips toward the hoop the way Wilt did
even then.

Bill would also emulate a certain move to the basket that
he saw Elgin Baylor make against the Hawks in nearby St.

*Willis Reed, Knick captain, goes down in the fifth
game and all, 'twas feared, was lost.* UPI

Louis. Bill would describe what he was doing, mimicking a sportscaster, as so many of us have done at one time or another. And there was the time he met Jerry West at a basketball clinic. Jerry showed him how he always bounced the ball extra hard just before he'd spring into the air for his jump shot, believing it helped catapult him higher. Ever since, Bill has bounced that last dribble just a bit harder.

When Bradley was growing up these players were something special to him. Now, as a New York Knick after a storied All-America career at Princeton and a stay as a Rhodes Scholar at Oxford, Bill felt compelled to remind people that "I'm not a kid anymore." That is, he would not stand and stare at the sight of Chamberlain, Baylor and West, all wearing the purple uniform of the Los Angeles Lakers, the Knicks' opponent in the title series of the NBA playoffs that concluded the 1969–70 season.

He was reminded of all that kid stuff when his folks had telephoned him a few nights earlier and his mother told him she'd found something he'd get a kick out of now, namely the Wilt Chamberlain scrapbook. Bradley had put away his childhood idolatry when he left Crystal City High School. Some men never do—like Lakers' owner Jack Kent Cooke, who collects the real thing, not just paste and paper images. A millionaire many times over, Cooke can indulge in such hobbies. Nearly two years earlier, Cooke was willing to meet the monumental salary demands of Chamberlain, then playing for the Philadelphia 76ers, so he sent several players to the 76ers and signed Chamberlain to a multiyear contract calling for between $150,000 and $175,000 a year.

Cooke couldn't have been happier. He thought he'd bought Los Angeles its first NBA title. So did a lot of other people. And no wonder. With West and Baylor already on the ball-

club, the Lakers now had three of the league's all-time greatest superstars—and three-fifths of the league's first-string All-
Star team. How could anyone beat them?

Five times since the Lakers had moved from Minneapolis
to Los Angeles, the team had been frustrated in the final
playoff round in its bid for the title. Each time the Boston
Celtics, led by Bill Russell, destroyed L.A.'s championship
dreams, usually in the seventh game of the series. It made it
all the harder to accept.

It was presumed that Chamberlain's presence in the pivot
would change that. On paper it did. But on the floor of The
Forum in Los Angeles in the spring of 1969 it did not. Russell
reached back once more, in a last hurrah before retiring from
the game, and rallied the Celtics, fourth-place finishers in the
regular season. The Lakers lost the big one once again. And
if Cooke cried in his pillow that night, he could be forgiven.

The Celtics couldn't survive the Russell retirement and they
didn't make it to the playoffs at the end of the 1969–70
season. Now it was the New York Knicks, a new challenger
on the block, in the best-of-seven for that elusive championship. For most of the season it seemed that Cooke's championship dreams were due for disappointment once more.
Chamberlain wrecked his knee early in the schedule and no
one expected him to return. But he did, in heroic fashion,
with a week remaining in the regular season, and he was the
key to the Lakers knocking off the Phoenix Suns and Atlanta
Hawks in the Western Division playoffs.

"Last year I thought we could go all the way," said Baylor.
"This year I wasn't sure until Wilt came back."

Baylor had been disappointed more often than any of the
Lakers, including Cooke. As a rookie with the Minneapolis
Lakers he was on the losing team in the championship series.

235

West was frustrated six times, Wilt three times. West, Baylor and Chamberlain stood 1-2-3 in career playoff scoring, but only Wilt had ever been on a title team—1967, with the Philadelphia 76ers.

The Knicks were new at this. Through the years they were lucky just making the playoffs, and hadn't made the final round since 1953, when they lost to the Minneapolis Lakers. Their franchise was frustration personified. Since the NBA was started twenty-four years earlier, the Knicks never had won the title. All season long they had been celebrated with cover stories in magazines that had never before paid pro basketball any mind. It started when the Knicks went on a record eighteen-game winning streak early in the season.

Besides Bradley, the Knicks' starting five was made up of Willis Reed, the NBA's MVP during the regular season; Walt Frazier, the fearless ball-thief and quarterback of the club; Dick Barnett, the lefty with the herky-jerky jump shot; and Dave DeBusschere, the brawny boardman and clutch shooter. And there were the supersubs, Cazzie Russell, Dave Stallworth and Mike Riordan, and there was Nate Bowman, a backstop for Reed when he rested.

The Lakers' lineup included rookie Dick Garrett and Keith Erickson, a starter on two NCAA championship teams at UCLA.

It would be some series. It would go the limit, seven games, but in retrospect the most sensational sizzler of them all was that memorable fifth game at the Garden. The 19,500 fans (the thirty-seventh sellout of the season. Attendance has since grown to at least a million judging by those who say they were there) who were there still don't believe it. And neither do most of the actors in what developed into living-theater drama.

New York, fresh from playoff victories over the Baltimore Bullets and Milwaukee Bucks, beat the Lakers in the first game at the Garden, 124–112. The Lakers came back to take the second, 105–103. The series then shifted to The Forum in the Los Angeles suburb of Inglewood, where there were two overtime contests. The Knicks won, 111–108, then lost, 121–115. Jerry West had sent the third game into overtime with a last-second 55-foot shot that stunned all who saw it. Commenting on the shot afterward, keenly disappointed because the Lakers lost anyway, Chamberlain philosophized, "Anything is possible."

The statement took on new meaning after the fifth meeting —the unbelievable fifth game they're still talking about in New York. The Lakers led from the start with Chamberlain coming on strong, making three baskets in less than 2 minutes as L.A. moved to an 11–4 advantage. Soon it was 25–15. And with 8 minutes gone the Knicks fell into deep trouble. Willis Reed, turning to drive down the left side of the lane for a layup, strained two muscles in his right thigh and dropped to the floor in distress, like a wounded buffalo. The jungle went quiet.

The big man twisted on the floor. The action moved up-court as he writhed in pain. Photographers moved in for a close-up of the grimace that twisted his mask.

"Oh, my God," groaned Reed as he rolled about.

"I was sick when I saw Willis," said DeBusschere. "You never give up, but inside you knew our chances were very slim."

Or none.

Frazier figured it was all over. "He had been the big man for us all year," said Walt. "I could see the championship going down the drain, man, down the drain."

237

Bradley was stunned. He knew Willis wouldn't leave the court unless he was in great pain. The thought crossed his mind that his dream of playing on a championship team might have collapsed with Reed.

Reed got up, tried to play for 8 seconds, and then was gone, the team trainer and doctor accompanying him to the locker room for treatment.

Without Reed, who had played a decisive role in every playoff game won by the Knicks, it all seemed hopeless. The big man was out. Nate Bowman moved onto the floor to take his place.

The Lakers, with Reed out of the game, were determined to get the ball to 7-foot-2 Chamberlain. The Knicks trailed by 10 when Reed went out and Chamberlain scored 7 of the Lakers' next 12 points and increased the lead to 37–24 before Knicks' coach Red Holzman benched Bowman in favor of Bill Hosket, a seldom-used sub.

The Knicks were still spastic. They appeared to be over-matched. The game got sloppy here, and nothing much happened. Hosket came out with the Lakers leading, 43–32, and with 4:31 to go in the second quarter, DeBusschere was told to guard Chamberlain, quite an assignment for a guy 6-6, even one as determined as DeBusschere. To Holzman's credit, he kept looking for a solution.

The two teams matched shots the remainder of the period and it was 53–40 at the intermission. The Lakers had once led by 16, 51–35, but the Knicks spurted at the end to close it to 13. Surprisingly enough, the Lakers outscored the Knicks by only 3 points in the second period.

There was still some hope that Reed would return in the second half. Dr. James Parkes had administered a shot of Novocaine and another of cortisone in hopes of getting the big guy ready. They shoot workhorses, don't they?

238

Normally an unemotional man, Coach Holzman made a brief speech that smacked of Notre Dame's dynamic Knute Rockne in all his "Win one for the Gipper" glory. "Let's win this one for Willis," said Holzman in the locker room. "He's won a lot of games for us. Let's win one for him."

The Knicks opened the third quarter with DeBusschere, Bradley, Frazier, Barnett and Russell on the floor. Holzman wanted to go with his best shooters. DeBusschere at 6-6, was the biggest of the bunch. When Mel Counts was in, the Lakers had two 7-footers. The Knicks chopped the lead to 58–53 after 4½ minutes of the third quarter, but then fell back by 11. At the end of the period they were behind, 82–75, and they certainly didn't look like winners.

Reed would not return to action, the Garden gathering was told, and there was a general sigh of despair in the place. Reed lay on a training table and listened to the public-address announcer in the dressing room.

In desperation the Knicks were scrambling all over the court, pressing with a drop-off defense, and they were using a 1-3-1 offense suggested by Bradley during the half. Frazier knew he was stealing the ball a lot, but he thought it meaningless, as the Lakers held the lead.

"We gambled," said Holzman. "Sometimes you get buried when you gamble."

Early in the fourth period, Frazier scored on a spinning lay-in. Stallworth, in for Russell, hit a short baseline jumper, and Bradley and Barnett both hit foul shots. Suddenly it was 84–81. DeBusschere picked up his fifth personal and sat down. Baylor hit two free throws for the Lakers, but Stallworth, now watching Wilt, hit a fall-away jumper and Barnett fired in a one-hander to bring the Knicks to within 1 point at 86–85. The Garden crowd kept chanting, "Let's go, Knicks!"

239

Over the Garden intercom "it sounded like fantasy," said Reed later.

Stallworth scored to tie the game at 89-all. Baylor hit on his second-straight shot to send the Lakers out front once more. But Barnett made two free throws and, when the Knicks got the ball on a turnover, they called a time-out.

John Havlicek, the captain of the Celtics, was sitting at courtside watching instead of playing for the championship. At the beginning of the third quarter, Havlicek said, "It will be a miracle if the Knicks come on to win this."

After they tied it at 91–91, Havlicek cried, "It's the greatest thing to watch the way they've come back. This team has a lot of heart." And as the Knicks put the ball into play, he added, "If they score this place will go nuts."

Bradley let loose a jumper from the top of the key. Swish. The Knicks were ahead for the first time all night. The place went nuts.

The outside shooters of the Knicks kept popping away until Wilt moved out, and then they'd drive around him, especially Stallworth and Russell. Russell was playing a great all-around game. Bradley and Stallworth, neither previously great in the series, couldn't be stopped.

Frazier hit the final shot to make it 107–100. Later Walt would say, "It was unreal."

"It had to be one of the greatest comebacks of all times," Havlicek said.

The Knicks had outscored the Lakers, 32–18, in the final period, a period in which they forced ten turnovers—for a game total of 30—while committing none themselves.

Even stranger, Chamberlain got three shots in the second half. West got two. "It was a very strange game," said West. "I'm not sure the Knicks could do that again."

*New York's Dave Stallworth, rising above the Lakers'
Jerry West and Wilt Chamberlain, was one of the
Knick heroes in the incredible game.* UPI

Who could? "They speeded it up like a fast movie," losing coach Joe Mullaney moaned.

"I still can't believe it," said Wilt.

The Knicks, not the Lakers now had the 3–2 edge in the series. Reed limped around the dressing room hugging the Knicks and thanking them for what they had done. He would miss the next game in Los Angeles and the Knicks would lose, but he would make a valiant return in the finale, and the Knicks would win, 113–99, to take their first NBA title, 4 games to 3.

None could match Monday's madness, however.

Mullaney comes to mind. His gray head hung back against the concrete wall as he stared at the ceiling outside his team's locker room.

"Unbelievable," Mullaney muttered to no one in particular. "Just unbelievable."

A priest standing at his side offered some consolation. "They believe in miracles here," he said.